Village U
— in —

KENT

Village Walks
in
KENT

Bea Cowan

COUNTRYSIDE BOOKS
NEWBURY, BERKSHIRE

First published 1998
Revised and reprinted 2000
© Bea Cowan 1998

COUNTRYSIDE BOOKS
3 Catherine Road
Newbury, Berkshire

To view our complete range of books,
please visit us at
www.countrysidebooks.co.uk

ISBN 1 85306 521 8

Designed by Graham Whiteman
Photographs by the author
Maps and illustrations by Trevor Yorke

Front Cover Photo showing the village
of Eynsford taken by Bill Meadows

Produced through MRM Associates Ltd., Reading
Printed by Woolnough Bookbinding Ltd., Irthlingborough

Contents

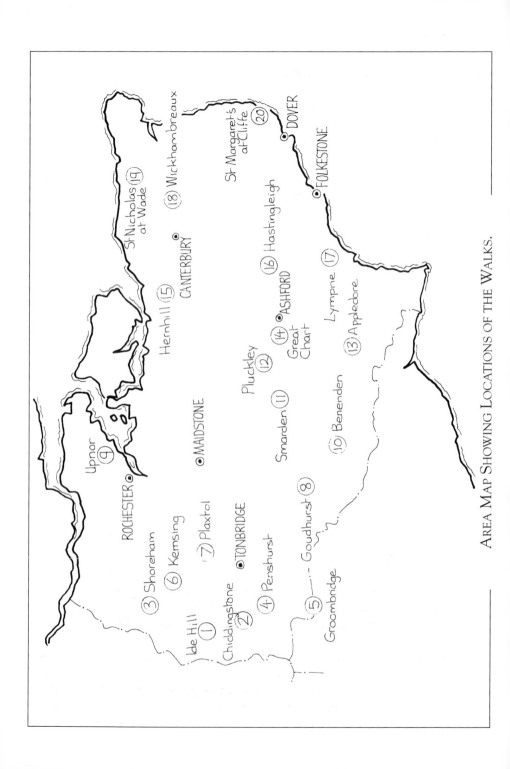

AREA MAP SHOWING LOCATIONS OF THE WALKS.

WALK

Publisher's Note

We hope that you obtain considerable enjoyment from this book; great care has been taken in its preparation. Although at the time of publication all routes followed public rights of way or permitted paths, diversion orders can be made and permissions withdrawn.

We cannot of course be held responsible for such diversion orders and any inaccuracies in the text which result from these or any other changes to the routes nor any damage which might result from walkers trespassing on private property. We are anxious though that all details covering the walks are kept up to date and would therefore welcome information from readers which would be relevant to future editions.

Introduction

The villages of Kent have histories as varied as the geography of the south-east. Some areas have seen settlers from early times. The river valleys, such as those of the Medway, the Darent and the Bourne, drew Stone Age men. Bronze Age settlers followed, then the early farmers, next the Celts, later the Romans. By the time the Saxons imposed their system of manors and the Church its parishes, some settlements were already growing. Other areas were settled later, the North Downs for crops and grazing, the Weald for its clearings (*dens*) in the forest, where swineherds brought their pigs to feed on the acorns. The High Weald, inaccessible with heavy clay and poor roads, remained remote for longer but even here clusters of farms grew around the clearings on the slopes. In all these places the settlements formed the beginnings of the villages you see today.

This collection of 20 walks takes the opportunity to explore just some of the many different Kent villages. Almost always, at the centre, you will find the church. It may well not be the original place of worship on the site. Early churches were frequently made of wood, later to be destroyed by fire. Sometimes, as at Appledore, the early building fell foul of raiders and invaders. On more than one occasion lightning led to their destruction. But villagers invariably took a pride in the church and a new building followed soon after. For this reason you will see embellishments and adornments in side chapels or memorials. Such accounts often add considerable human interest to the history of church and neighbourhood.

Then there is the inn, which, in many places, has stood on the same site for several hundred years. Sometimes private dwellings when first built, sometimes an alehouse from the start, these centres today, as in the past, provide a focal point for the neighbourhood. Nearby are the houses and you will often find, in the districts chosen for these walks, marvellous examples of the architecture for which Kent is famous: the half-timbered houses, the fine brick buildings made with the different-coloured bricks from local clays, the hung tiles and the weatherboarding. You will always find a view and a chance to enjoy the countryside which gave each village its particular characteristic. Today the pattern of the countryside continues to change, especially the field patterns, as hedges and orchards are uprooted and large expanses for cereal take their place. But always you will find the basic pattern, the patchwork of fields, the woodland and the shaws or shelter belts.

The life-blood of any village is its inhabitants, and Kent has an abundance of villagers who really care for their environment. Therefore, readers are asked to respect their way of life and to use the utmost discretion when parking vehicles. Car parking locations are indicated in the text – but if these are full, or for some reason unusable, please ensure that you park your vehicle in such a way as not to be a nuisance to those who live close by. Some of the walks commence from the village inn where, it must be stressed, parking is only for patrons. If you are having food and drink there, however, your vehicle can probably remain parked while you walk - but please ask the landlord first.

Sources of refreshment are included for each walk, together with the telephone numbers of the pubs so that you can establish their opening times. Places of interest within striking distance of each featured village are also given, to help you plan a full day out if you wish.

The walks are circular, starting from the village itself, or, occasionally, a suitable point close by. All use well-established rights of way. Some walks make use of the long distance paths which cross Kent such as the Saxon Shore Way, the Greensand Way, the North Downs Way. Others use the medium distance paths such as the Eden Valley Walk or the walk along the Royal Military Canal. Others touch some of the circular paths maintained by the County Council or the Local District. A few take you along rights of way less well used. A prime objective has been to provide direct, no-nonsense route descriptions for each walk, coupled with a clear sketch map. For those requiring more detail, the relevant OS Landranger (1:50,000) and Pathfinder (1:25,000) map numbers are given. The former, smaller scale sheets cover a wider area but the latter are by far the more interesting and useful for the walker. I hope that, with good shoes or boots and, perhaps, a walking stick to help you push back the occasional bramble, you will derive as much pleasure from these walks as we have done.

I should like to thank all those who have helped me to prepare this selection, especially those from Kent County Council and from the borough and parish councils who have walked and marked the footpaths before me. Finally I would like to thank my husband for his support, company and interest throughout the project and my cousin, Mary Ingram, for her company and help.

Bea Cowan

IDE HILL

Length: 4 miles

Getting there: Ide Hill is 2¼ miles south of the A25 from Brasted, and 3 miles north-east of the junction of the B2027/B2042 at Four Elms.	Parking: A useful small car park lies below the village on the B2042. There is some parking beside the road from Sundridge and around The Green (limited).	Maps: OS Landranger 188; Explorer 147 or Pathfinder 1208 (GR 487518).

Ide Hill, high on the Greensand Ridge, has all the ingredients of the traditional village, with church, weatherboarded houses and pub, all set round a spacious village green. It acquired its name, *Edythshyll*, in Anglo-Saxon times but for centuries it remained little more than manorial wastes. While a line of prosperous farms grew up on the lower slopes, swineherds drove their pigs to and from the Wealden clearings in their search for pannage and rarely stopped at Ide Hill for long. Gradually, however, settlers remained and by the 17th century had created a reasonable-sized hamlet. A chapel, consecrated in 1807, meant that villagers no longer had to walk to church in Sundridge. The present church, St Mary's, with shingled spire, was built in 1865. Villagers dug the well, said to be 'as deep as the church is tall', in 1900 during a time of drought, so setting the seal on this remote and attractive green.

The walk takes you down the slopes of the Greensand Ridge and over farmland, passed Chains Farm and Henden Manor, two of those farms which prospered in the late Middle Ages. At Henden you can still see the line of its moat. Henry VIII is said to have stayed here on his way to visit Anne Boleyn at Hever Castle. You then return up the slopes over farmland and through woodland, and climb to Toys Hill, the highest point in Kent, before returning over pasture and arable land to Ide Hill. Throughout the walk you have extensive views over the Weald of Kent. Traces of woodland, damaged in the storm of 1987, still remain but much has now regrown.

THE WALK

❶ Take the tarmac driveway to the right of St Mary's church. Continue ahead along a sandy track to a field. Bear left downhill, following the Greensand Way sign. Turn left and walk to a low marker pointing right. Follow this down to the road to a

small car park. Continue ahead for 50 yards then turn right across the road and follow a metalled drive for 20 yards. Turn left uphill to a clearing, then take the right-hand track downhill. Turn left along a metalled track round and downhill to a cottage, Boarhill. Turn right towards the left of its garage then cross a stile to follow footpath SR 246. Go ahead along a clearly trodden path, continuing along the lower slope of the field just above the fenceline. Below you see the reservoir at Bough Beech, formed from the river Eden and now an important wildlife site. Take the left-hand track of two, cross a stile and follow a broad farm track down the right-hand side of a field, bearing left to a gate and stile. Cross the stile, go through a gate, leave a house to your left, then continue up the drive to the road.

❷ Cross the road and turn left. After 100 yards turn right along a private road to Henden Manor. When you reach this moated manor house, walk ahead through two sets of wooden gates, between farm buildings. After 175 yards turn right at a double-fronted house. Walk along a concrete farm track. Cross a stile beside a

The village pub.

metal gate, then bear left downhill to trees and a stream. Cross a field bridge. Cross a stile to the left of a metal gate. Bear right. Walk along the field headland with woodland on your right for 120 yards. Where the woodland swings right, bear left across the field to a gap in the hedge. Cross a field bridge and continue up the next field to the treeline. Cross first a wooden bridge then a stile. Walk uphill, between trees. Bear left to a metal gate. After 10 yards turn right over a stile. Follow the path between trees to the road. Turn right.

❸ After 110 yards turn right over a stile. Bear left up the slope and make for a gate set below a white house with an oast. Cross a stile beside the gate then walk to the fence ahead. Go through a small wicket gate. Cross a house drive then continue along a metalled track. Cross a stile above a pond. Continue along a narrow path until you reach the corner of a house. Here turn left and walk uphill between fences. Turn right onto a driveway, then left and walk up to a T junction. Climb the steps ahead then continue uphill to a marker post with yellow arrows. To reach the Fox and Hounds, turn left to the road, then right. The Fox and Hounds is 175 yards further on.

❹ To return to Ide Hill, turn right at the marker post. Leave the post to your right if you are returning from the pub. Walk downhill, going ahead at cross-tracks. Cross a stile into a field. Turn left and follow the headland along the top of the

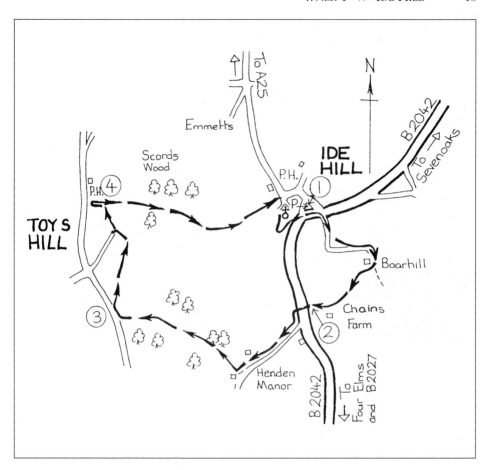

field. Bear right downhill, going over two stiles to reach a stockproof bridge in the far right-hand corner of the lower field. Cross this, then walk up a headland, leaving the fence immediately to your left. Continue ahead uphill, going over three stiles, then walk on, following the same line, to return to Ide Hill village.

CHIDDINGSTONE

Length: 5 miles, with a shorter option of 2½ miles

Getting there: Chiddingstone lies 6½ miles west of Tonbridge, 1½ miles south of the B2027 at Bough Beech.	Parking: Parking space may be found on either side of the village street and outside the Castle Inn.	Maps: OS Landranger 188; Explorer 147 or Pathfinder 1228 (GR 501452).

With half-timbered, jettied houses, and with the fine, sandstone church of St Mary at the centre, Chiddingstone, owned by the National Trust, still looks much as it did in medieval times, just a few houses along a short main street. Small though it always has been, Chiddingstone played its part in the history of Kent and England. One 15th-century half-timbered house was occupied by Roger Attwood, a supporter of a rebellion led by Jack Cade which touched the whole of Kent. The building that houses the post office, first mentioned in 1453, was later bought by Sir Thomas Boleyn, father of Anne Boleyn, herself the second wife of Henry VIII. Anne Boleyn is recalled in Chiddingstone Castle where some wood panelling is said to have come from her bedstead at nearby Hever Castle where she grew up.

The walk takes you from the village centre over open fields and through woodland typical of the High Weald. You have many glorious views of this rolling countryside. You walk beside several of the steep-sided ghylls rich in the plant life which characterises this area and you see some huge outcrops of sandstone which normally lie under the Wealden clay. On your return you pass Chiddingstone Castle, never a true castle but a country house built in 17th-century style on the site of the old manor house, with Gothic battlements added a century later.

THE WALK

❶ With the Castle Inn on your right, walk along the village street for 200 yards. Just after a small green on your right, turn right through a kissing gate and follow a sandy path, crossing two stiles. Bear right downhill along a field path to a stile beside trees. Cross the stile, turn left and continue to an old kissing gate. Bear left. Go through a wooden swing gate and continue through woodland. After 200 yards take the left-hand fork and continue to the road. Turn right.

❷ For the shorter walk, continue along the road for ½ mile, then turn right over a stile at point 4 and continue.

For the full walk, turn left after 75 yards. Follow a footpath across a field to a stile in the far right-hand corner. Cross, then turn left along a metalled lane, and continue to farm buildings and a house at Wat Stock. Turn right and continue along a metalled track for ½ mile. Where the main track turns left at Salman's Farm, walk ahead along a narrow, grass path leaving a garden fence on your right. Turn right and walk for 30 yards to the entrance to Salman's Manor. Turn left and walk along a metalled drive. Just after the drive turns left, double back uphill into woodland at 350 degrees, then turn left to follow a fairly steep woodland path up to a road.

❸ Turn right and walk for 500 yards to a right-hand bend. Here turn right, go down steps, then follow a path below woodland. Cross a stile. Walk downhill over pasture towards a vineyard on the far slope. Cross a stockproof bridge, and continue towards woods. Negotiate two more bridges, going first ahead, then right. Continue along a

The Chiding Stone is located just south of the village.

woodland path to a field corner. Walk up the left-hand side of a vineyard. Turn left when you reach an upper field of vines. Continue between trees and follow the footpath beside a poplar plantation. Join a gravel drive and follow this to a stile beside a gate. Cross the stile and walk up the right-hand side of two fields. Cross a stile and follow a narrow lane between a garden fence and trees. Leave a garage to your right and continue along a broad gravel track for 100 yards. Opposite Oakenden Farm turn right up steps, cross a stile and follow the path along the top of a field. At the end of a line of trees turn left over a stile. Follow a narrow path between a hedge and a post-and-rail fence. Just after a large outcrop of Wealden sandstone, bear left, uphill, along a sandy track. At the road turn

right and walk between sandstone blocks and hanging beeches to Hoath Corner. You now come to a delightful group of 16th-century buildings which happily includes the Rock public house. From here continue along the road for ½ mile

❹ Turn left over a stile opposite a house and walk down the left-hand side of a field beside a line of trees. Cross a stile and bear right down a broad farm track. Where the track swings left turn right up a broad grass track. Continue between trees, leaving a pond to your right. Cross a stile into a field, then turn left along the headland beside trees. When the trees end bear right across the field. Bear left round a large reed-lined pond. Cross two stiles, then follow a concrete farm track through Hill Hoath

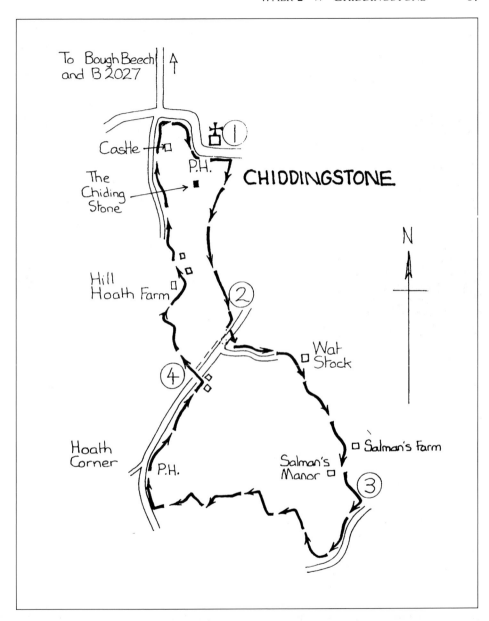

Farm. Turn right along a small road to pass the entrance to Chiddingstone Castle after ½ mile. Turn right at the crossroads and follow the road round to Chiddingstone village.

SHOREHAM

Length: 4½ miles

Getting there: Shoreham is ¾ mile west of the A225 between Farningham and Sevenoaks, 3½ miles south of the A20 at Farningham.	Parking: There is a well-signed car park at the top of the village in Filston Lane. Parking is allowed along the village street.	Maps: OS Landranger 188; Explorer 147 or Pathfinder 1192 (GR 518616).

Shoreham lies beside the river Darent, a small village beside a river crossing. Its name, from Anglo-Saxon *Scieran*, to cleave, reflects the way the river cuts its course beneath a slope of the North Downs. Shoreham has mainly grown up since medieval times, its economy based on the pasture beside the river. As you walk down Church Street, the church of St Peter and St Paul behind you, the steep slope of the North Downs ahead, you see many half-timbered houses dating from Tudor times. Beside the river are Georgian and Victorian houses, reminders of a period when Shoreham provided a quiet retreat, for even when the road along the slopes above Shoreham was turnpiked the village remained little frequented by visitors. The bridge makes a focal point. From here you can see the clear chalk stream of the Darent as it tumbles over flints and stones. Beside the bridge stands a war memorial. Through the trees you can make out another, a large white cross cut into the hillside above.

The walk takes you beside the river and across fields and past the site of Shoreham's castle. At Lullingstone Park, for centuries the deer park belonging to Lullingstone Castle, you climb above the valley and walk through woodland, first through an area planted in the 18th century, then through old coppice. As you return to Shoreham along the upper slopes above the Darent, you see the valley stretch ahead and below you, then look down on Shoreham itself, before a last steep drop to the village.

FOOD and DRINK

Shoreham once had many inns. Now few remain but they are well worth visiting. The Olde George (telephone: 01959 522017), opposite the church, offers a range of real ales, two permanent, two guest, changing regularly. The Kings Arms (telephone: 01959 523100), west of the bridge in Church Street, also offers good ales. This inn is distinguished by its ostler (model only), still awaiting your arrival in his box in the wall. Inside the welcome is real. En route, teas and light snacks are available at Lullingstone Park Visitor Centre.

THE WALK

❶ From the car park turn right, then right again and walk down Church Street. Cross the bridge over the river Darent, then turn left and follow the riverside path. Just after Flint Cottage you pass The Water House where the artist Samuel Palmer lived from 1827 to 1834/5. Leave this house to your right and continue, first with houses, then fields, on your right. When you come to a hedge ahead of you, turn left and cross the river by a small bridge. Turn right and pass the weir. Continue along the track beside the river. Go through a wooden kissing gate and continue along a field headland.

At the next hedgeline bear left. Continue across a farm track, then cross a field to a gap between trees. Walk along a farm track above a large hop garden. When you reach a narrow road walk ahead, passing Castle Farm on your right. Where the road turns right, bear left into Lullingstone Park.

❷ From the car park at the Visitor Centre take the left-hand path into the park. To visit Lullingstone Castle, follow the Darent Valley footpath sign ahead, and continue beside the river Darent for ½ mile. For the main walk, go uphill, leaving the post and rail fence to your left. At the top continue into the woodland. Bear left at marker 3. Ignoring the many side tracks, continue ahead along the main path. Turn left at a wooden finger post and go through a gate,

following public footpath 206. Continue between a wooden fence and a tall hedge. Cross a stile into a field. Continue ahead, leaving a fence to your right.

PLACES of INTEREST

The **Visitor Centre at Lullingstone Park** (telephone: 01322 865995) has displays of local wildlife and an account of the history of this important park. **Lullingstone Castle** opens its house and grounds between April and September on some days (telephone: 01322 862114). To the south-east of Eynsford (north up the A225) you can reach **Lullingstone Roman Villa**, a remarkable example of Romano-British occupation in the valley, with bath house, hypocaust and, above all, superb mosaics (telephone: 01322 863467).

View of the Darent Valley.

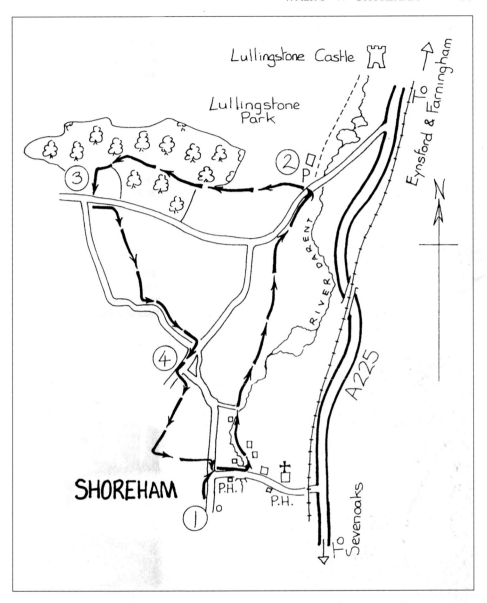

❸ Cross a stile and go down steps to the road. Turn left and walk for 100 yards. At the bend in the road take the public footpath to the right and walk along a metalled farm track. Swing left past a small white house then bear right past a garage along a grassy lane. Continue along a field headland, leaving a hedge to your right. Cross a stile from where you have a good view southwards. Bear left and follow the field edge downhill to a road. Turn left. Walk for 400 yards, then turn right at a junction, following the sign towards Halstead and Chelsfield.

❹ Ignoring a left fork in the road, continue for 250 yards, then turn left along a broad track above and to the right of a narrower footpath. Continue for 30 yards, then turn right at a barrier and climb steadily, following a broad track above the valley. Ignoring a right-hand turn into woodland, turn left after 800 yards. Go down steps, then continue down a chalky path. Cross a stile and walk down the left-hand side of a field. At the bottom of the field turn left over a stile, then immediately right. Walk down a lane between hedges and fence. Go through a kissing gate then continue past a playing field and tennis courts to the road. Turn right to return to the car park, making a left turn down Church Street if you want to return to the village centre.

PENSHURST

Length: 2¾ miles

Getting there: Penshurst lies 5 miles west of Tonbridge. To reach it, take the B2176 from the A26, 1½ miles south of Tonbridge; alternatively, leave Hildenborough, west of Tonbridge, by the B2027, then take the B2188 just west of Leigh.

Parking: There is space for some parking beside the road, especially just north of the village. There is also a good car park for patrons of the Leicester Arms, and another for visitors to Penshurst Place.

Maps: OS Landranger 188; Explorer 147 or Pathfinder 1228 (GR 527438).

Penshurst lies on the edge of the High Weald, beside the river Medway, the last village before the river emerges onto the Wealden plain. Typical of many English villages, its church and manor house stand side by side. The church of St John the Baptist, first built in the 13th century, dominates the skyline with pinnacles on its sandstone tower. The manor house, Penshurst Place, stands just north of the village. In 1338, Sir John de Pulteney, draper, merchant and four times Mayor of London, bought the manor from the de Penchester family. He engaged Edward

FOOD and DRINK

There are several opportunities for refreshment here. The Leicester Arms, part of the Leicester estate from the early 17th century to 1921, is open all day every day (telephone: 01892 870551). Here you will find, among other good ales, the local Larkins ale brewed at Chiddingstone. You can eat in the restaurant as well as in the bar. Nearby are Quaintways Tea Rooms (open daily) and Fir Tree House Tea Rooms. A restaurant is open for visitors to Penshurst Place.

III's master craftsman, Edward Hurley, and built a house to seal his reputation. The Great Hall at the centre, well lit by windows in the roof, is one of the most remarkable to survive. In 1552 Edward VI granted the manor to Sir William Sidney, grandfather of Sir Philip Sidney, the poet. That family has lived at Penshurst Place ever since. In 1618 Sir William's other grandson, Robert, already created Viscount Lisle, received the earldom of Leicester for his services to king and country. Much of the history is told in the monuments within the church.

The walk starts in Leicester Square, just south of St John's churchyard. Here two Tudor cottages flank a third, raised on posts to form an arched gateway, In 1850 the architect, George Devey, added two more in the same style to complete this delightful corner. You see more of Devey's embellishments in the Tudor-style gateway to the entrance to Penshurst Place and in the stone bridge over the river Medway. From Penshurst Place you walk to open country. A climb to heathland above the village brings fine views first of the village, then of Penshurst Place, in the valley setting.

THE WALK

❶ With the archway and the church behind you, turn left out of Leicester Square and walk along the road to the large archway at the entrance to Penshurst Place and Gardens, following the signs to Killick's Bank and Ensfield. For a while you will also follow the Eden Valley Walk route. Walk past the wall of Penshurst Place. Leave a small lake to your left, then continue ahead on a concrete farm path for 500 yards. Turn left through the first of many stiles typical of the Penshurst estate, curved like the outer prongs of the pitchfork used in the quartering of the Leicester Arms. Turn right immediately, and walk up the right-hand side of a field. After 100 yards cross another stile then bear left to the top of the field, from where you have a superb view back over Penshurst. Pass a marker post and continue to a stile in the fence.

❷ Turn left just before the stile and follow a broad grass track with trees on your left above pasture. Go through a forked stile and continue along a broad farm track. Where the path reveals old tarmac go through a stile to the left of a gate, then

PLACES of INTEREST

If you have time you should not miss seeing **Penshurst Place and Gardens**, open daily from the end of March to the end of September (telephone: 01892 870307). In addition to Edward Hurley's Great Hall are rooms built from Tudor and Elizabethan times. The Buckingham Building, from about 1430, houses interesting state rooms. The Long Gallery, Sir Robert Sidney's development, holds a number of family portraits. There is also an intriguing toy museum.

One of the Tudor cottages seen from the churchyard.

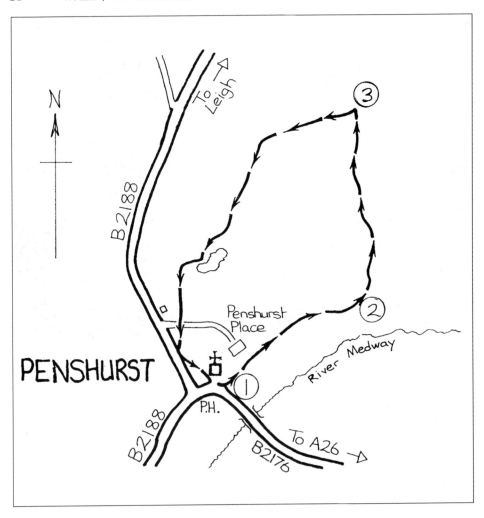

walk through a short stretch of woodland. Cross another stile and walk up the right-hand side of a large field, leaving a fence to your right. At the top of the field continue ahead over heathland until you join a broad swathe of short grass just beyond a wedge of woodland.

❸ Turn left. You can now see the Ashdown Forest on the horizon to the south-west. Continue along a broad swathe of heathland grass for 600 yards. Pass first an old gate post on your right then a little-used stile. Bear left, following the same broad path. Penshurst Place lies below and ahead of you between the trees. Walk steadily downhill. Go through a forked stile then follow a yellow arrow on a post, going downhill between trees towards a lake. Just before the lake bear right to a forked stile.

The entrance to Penshurst Place.

Go through this and walk ahead. Where the fence bends left, walk ahead then go through to a narrow gate. Pass a pillbox and an amazingly gnarled, hollow oak on your right. Walk past a house, then cross the main driveway to Penshurst Place, going through forked stiles on either side, and bear right to a stile. At the stile turn back at 45 degrees and follow the trodden path diagonally across the field to the far right-hand side, heading towards the church, to the right of Penshurst Place.

Go into the churchyard between the forked bars and follow the path round the west end of St John's church. Walk under the archway topped by the Tudor cottage and return to Leicester Square.

GROOMBRIDGE

Length: 3½ miles

Getting there: Groombridge lies on the B2110, 4 miles west of Tunbridge Wells and 5 miles north of Crowborough.	Parking: There is room for a few cars beside The Green in Old Groombridge or you may use the Crown's car park if you are visiting the pub. The best place, however, is the car park	south of the river Grom. Maps: OS Landranger 188; Explorer 18 or Pathfinder 1248 (GR 531375).

Old Groombridge traces its history to Saxon times when, as *Gromenbregge* (the bridge over the river Grom), it defended the frontier between Sussex and Kent. A sandstone bridge still marks the county boundary. The village grew from the mid-19th century when the London, Brighton and South Coast Railway brought a branch line here but its old heart remains intact, a cluster of 16th and 17th-century houses beside the green. Weatherboarded and with hung tiles, they make a picturesque group. In the 18th century the Crown, above The Green, became the headquarters of the Groombridge gang, smugglers even more violent and notorious than those from Hawkhurst. Over the road, the church of St John was built as a thanks-offering for the safe return of Prince Charles from Spain in 1625, the year he later became King. Nearby stands Groombridge Place, a moated manor house, where Richard Waller brought Charles, Duc d'Orleans as hostage after the battle of Agincourt. Philip Packer, a founder member of the Royal Society, rebuilt the house in 1662 to the finest standards of the day.

This walk takes you from the green, along the slopes above the river Grom. The route has some spectacular views, first of the valley where the tiny river carves its way towards the Medway, then of the Medway valley itself and the Ashdown Forest beyond. As you walk you see the soil change from the clay of the valley which once, at nearby Ashurst, yielded iron ore for cannon for the Navy. Higher up is sandstone where you walk between heathland trees before returning to the green of Old Groombridge

THE WALK

❶ Leave the green by the north-west corner and follow the narrow road uphill. Soon you pass, to your left, Court Lodge, a house with an intriguing past. Although

first built in the 15th century, it is a relative newcomer to the area as it was transported 30 miles from Udimore near Rye and rebuilt here in 1912. After 550 yards bear left over a stile. From here you can see the Medway valley stretching into the distance, with the Ashdown Forest to the south. On the slope below lies Burrswood, built by Decimus Burton for David Salomons in the 1830s when he was High Sheriff of Kent. The house is now a Christian Centre for Healing. Walk ahead across a field to a fence, go over a stile in the middle of trees and cross a small road. Climb up a short flight of steps. Cross another stile, then follow the path between trees. Cross a stile into a field, then follow the path downhill towards more trees. Cross a stile, then continue downhill. Cross two more stiles, then bear right across a field towards a stile in the right-hand corner.

❷ Cross into a shaw, then go over two more stiles a short distance apart. Walk up the right-hand side of a field for 150 yards. Cross a stile in the fence to your right. Bear left, and continue uphill. Cross a stile beside the fence, then continue ahead

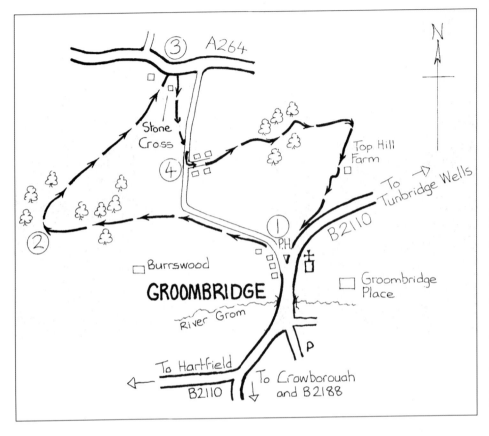

along the upper side of the field, keeping the same heading across two fields to a stile in the far left-hand corner. Leave a garden and tennis court to your right and walk along a lane to the road beside the entrance to Stone Cross.

❸ Turn right and walk along the road for 100 yards. When you reach the end of the garden fence of Stone Cross Lodge turn right over a stile into a field. Bear left downhill to a gate in the far side of a field beside woods. Cross a stile into woodland and bear left. Walk for 20 yards, then turn right and follow the path uphill. Go

through a swing gate at the top, then turn right along the road beside East Lodge and continue for 300 yards.

❹ Turn left at Keepers Cottage. Walk along a sandy driveway, first flanked by cottages, then with woodland on your left. Follow the path as it leads into woodland recently coppiced, then continue into mature woodland. When you emerge from trees continue along a hedged farm track. To your left you see Fernchase Manor, until recently known as Ashurst Place, an imposing white stucco building built in the 1830s. Turn right after 400 yards.

Groombridge Place.

When you reach a field walk ahead, leaving the fence to your right, then continue along a concrete farm track. Where the track bears left to Top Hill Farm, turn right, then, almost immediately, left. Walk down the left-hand side of a field. At the bottom, cross a stile and follow the clearly trodden path downhill. Turn right when you reach the road and walk for another 250 yards to The Green at Groombridge.

KEMSING

Length: 2½ miles

Getting there: From the A225 ½ mile east of Otford, turn off on the bend of the road and follow the road named the Pilgrims' Way East, signed to Kemsing. After 1 mile, take the 5th road on your right, Childsbridge Lane. Turn left after another ¼ mile following the sign to Heaversham, then continue for another ½ mile to the centre of Kemsing.

Parking: There is a good car park in Kemsing, immediately to the east of the Wheatsheaf pub, with toilets and nappy changing facilities.

Maps: OS Landranger 188; Explorer 147 or Pathfinder1208 (GR 555587).

Kemsing, high on the slopes of the North Downs, has a history dating from at least Saxon times. The village has spread to the west in this century and only a small part recalls its earliest days. St Edith's Well, in the centre of old Kemsing, is one survivor.

A convent stood here in the Middle Ages, where in the 10th century Edith, daughter of the Saxon King Edgar, spent her childhood. Her presence was said to hallow the well at its centre. The well became known for its healing powers and pilgrims used to that too is long gone. Today, in the road stretching past St Edith's Well, are houses from the prosperous days of sheep farming. Houses still stand with their timber framing exposed or with the hung tiles and brick understorey the wealthier people introduced for extra warmth and protection.

The centre of the old village makes an admirable starting place for a walk on the slopes of the North Downs. A climb through woods and up fields gives rewarding views over the valley below. On the top is a good pub to quench your thirst, while on your return you walk above Kemsing Down, a nature reserve where you

visit on their way to Canterbury. A castle also stood here, in King John's time, but

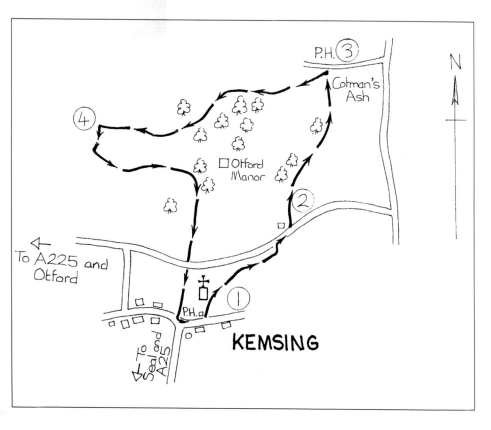

Some of the delightful cottages to be seen in the village.

find those trees and plants that evoke our past and are typical of the chalk downs, the wayfaring tree, wild spindle, dog rose, black bryony and traveller's joy. Harebells and common centaury grow in the grassland, and orchids nestle in the woods.

THE WALK

❶ From the car park turn left along the High Street and walk to Church Lane. Turn left beside the Vicarage. Just before the lychgate to St Mary's church, turn right into the common field. Bear left up the field, heading towards the right-hand side of a seat set against the top hedgeline. When you reach the road, the old Pilgrims' Way, follow the path which now runs beside it between trees. At a junction of tracks go down a couple of steps. Turn

left then right at the road and walk for 120 yards.

❷ Turn left into the entrance of Woodlea. Cross a stile to the right of a gate and walk up the path, first between a stone wall and a fence, then through woodland. Cross a stile into a field, then bear left uphill towards trees. Cross

---

PLACES of INTEREST

About 5 miles away, east of Sevenoaks, lies **Knole**, the largest private house in the country (National Trust). Built in the late 15th century and enlarged in the early 17th century, it contains paintings by Gainsborough and Van Dyck and houses a fine collection of 17th-century furniture (telephone: 01732 450608).

another stile. Follow the path, still climbing, through a shaw to another stile. Cross into a field, then continue uphill to the right-hand corner. Walk between trees to a stile then turn right along the North Downs Way. After 80 yards turn left over a stile. Walk up the left-hand side of a field. Cross a stile, then continue ahead along the right-hand side of two fields, crossing stiles, to reach a road.

❸ Turn left past the Rising Sun. After 100 yards bear left along a narrow path. Cross a stile. Walk along the left-hand side of a field. Cross a stile, then go ahead, first across a dog-leg of a field, then beside a fence, to a stile leading you into Fab's Wood. Follow a woodland path to a stile, cross into a broad field, then bear left and walk across a broad field for 350 yards. You now reach a free-standing stile whose only purpose now is as a landmark. Here bear right to a genuine stile, cross and walk towards two tall posts beside woodland. Go between the posts, turn right and walk

along a broad farm track. To your left is a driveway leading to Otford Manor (once Hildenborough Hall, and now an expedition centre). When you emerge from the woods, turn left over a stile, then right along the driveway.

❹ At the end of the drive, just after gateposts, turn left to follow part of the North Downs Way. Go downhill beside woodland. At cross-tracks bear left above Whiteleaf Down. Enter woods and cross a stile. As you emerge from the woods bear left to follow the North Downs Way uphill towards more woodland. At a junction of tracks turn right and walk downhill to a kissing gate at the edge of the woods. Follow a steep path downhill, go through a kissing gate then continue down steps to a road. Cross the road and follow the metalled footpath ahead of you to the road just above St Edith's Road, by the well. Turn left to return to the Wheatsheaf and the car park.

PLAXTOL

Length: 3½ miles

Getting there: Plaxtol is 6½ miles east of Sevenoaks, ½ mile east of the A227 and 1½ miles south of Ightham.	Parking: You will find a small car park at the top of the village. There is some parking space beside the road as well as car parks beside the pubs.	Maps: OS Landranger 188; Explorer 147 or Pathfinder 1209 (GR 603536).

To visit Plaxtol is to see the village in its setting in a valley. This is Greensand country where the soil has long been renowned for its fertility. Today the gentle, south-facing slopes bear apple orchards and cobnut platts. In every direction you see oast houses, reminder of times when hops grew here. Settlers have come here since the earliest times. Romans built villas nearby and left a cemetery. Not far away stands one of the oldest manor houses in Kent, Old Soar, once home of one of the extensive Culpeper family. A Georgian farmhouse replaced the Great Hall but the chapel and solar remain. Plaxtol itself grew up from Anglo-Saxon days on the site where young people gathered for sport and recreation, the *plaistow*, or play place of the area. At the centre stands Plaxtol church. This church has no dedication as it was built during the time of Cromwell and his Parliamentarians. Next to it stands 18th-century Church Row, built on a ragstone foundation, with weatherboarding of elm. To the south-west lies Fairlawne House, first built in the 14th century on land where the village fair was held in medieval times. The present house replaced the earlier one in the early 18th century.

This walk starts northward from the village, then leads you down to the river Bourne, a small but strong tributary of the Medway. You pass several old houses, usually farms in former times. You walk gently uphill again to Old Soar Manor, where you can see the two-storey solar block of the 13th-century manor house. As you return you see new orchards as well as old. Nearby, 19th-century archaeologists found a statue of the Roman goddess Minerva. Beside the river Bourne you pass the site where until recently mills produced high-quality paper, much in demand for bank notes and postal orders.

THE WALK

❶ Turn right out of the car park opposite the school. Ignore The Street to your right and walk up to the war memorial. Leave Plaxtol church to your left and walk up Tree Lane. Pass the small triangle of grass at the top of Grange Hill on your right and continue for another 150 yards. Turn right over a stile and walk down the right-hand side of the field ahead, with a hedge to your right. Ahead on the far slope you can see the oasts beside Old Soar Manor. At the end of the hedgeline, continue on the same line, making for a stile at the bottom of the field. You see to your right The Grange, built in baroque style in the early 18th century.

❷ Cross the stile onto a narrow road, then walk ahead, down Dux Hill. To your left lies the site of the Roman cemetery. At a T junction cross the stile set just to your right in the fence opposite. Walk down the left-hand side of a field and cross a bridge over the river Bourne. Walk up the right-hand side of the next field to a stile set 10 yards to the left of a large beech tree. Cross and follow the path along the slope ahead, making for the houses to the right of the three oasts. Cross a broad farm

PLACES of INTEREST

At **Old Soar Manor** (National Trust) you can see the solar and the chapel of this 13th-century knight's dwelling. There is also an exhibition. At **Ightham Mote** (also National Trust), near Ivy Hatch, you can see a moated manor house with 14th-century Great Hall and Chapel, as well as later additions built round a courtyard. (For each ring: 01732 811145.)

Old Soar Manor.

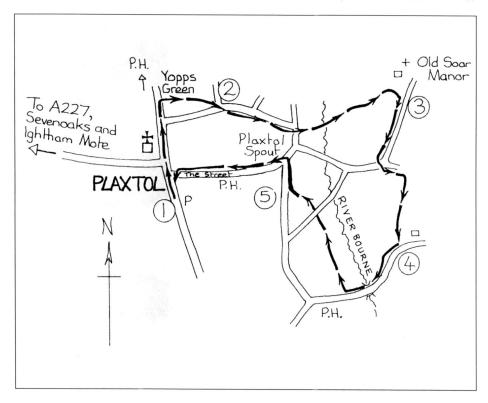

track and continue to a stile set in a poplar hedge. Cross the stile into a small field. Walk ahead, leaving farm buildings to your left. Go through a swing gate in the far left-hand corner of the field, and go down steps to the road. To reach Old Soar, which lies 60 yards further on, with its own signed entrance beyond the first large gate, turn left up the road.

❸ To continue the walk, turn right at the road beyond the swing gate (go straight on if you are coming from Old Soar) and walk for 700 yards down Old Soar Lane. Where the road turns right go ahead over a stile into an orchard. Turn left and walk for 200 yards, leaving the hedge on your left. Turn

right beside a gate and walk along a broad farm track, first past apple trees, then past soft fruit. Go ahead at cross-tracks, leaving a line of tall trees to your left. Continue between a tall hedge on your left and a windbreak on your right, leaving Rough-way House to your left.

❹ Turn right at the road and continue downhill until you reach Roughway Bridge. Walk on for another 100 yards. Here you may go ahead along the road to reach the Kentish Rifleman after ¼ mile. To continue the walk, turn right (left if you are coming from the pub) along a narrow lane. The paper mills for which the area was well-known stood, until recently, beside the river Bourne to your right. Go over one stile halfway down the lane, then cross another leading into a field. Walk ahead across one field. In the next field walk 10 yards to the right of a marker post, going over a sleepered walkway, an important feature in wet weather. Continue to the road. Cross the road, then cross another stile into a field and walk ahead, leaving trees to your right. After 250 yards bear left and cross to the far left-hand corner of the field. Cross a stile beside a gate, then turn right.

❺ Here you may turn left after 20 yards and follow a lane which emerges halfway up The Street. Otherwise continue for 350 yards to Plaxtol Spout, so called because a spring emerges here from the greensand. Here you pass the fine half-timbered, 14th-century Spout House, home for a while of Hyder's Forge. Turn left to walk up The Street. At the top of The Street turn left to reach the car park.

GOUDHURST

Length: 3 miles

Getting there: Goudhurst lies on the A262, 8½ miles west of Bidenden and 3 miles east of the A21 north of Lamberhurst.

Parking: A small car park lies 200 yards south of the crossroads, beside the B2079. The Star and Eagle has its own car park reached by a side road

from the B2079.

Maps: OS Landranger 188; Explorer 136 or Pathfinder 1249 (GR 724722).

At nearly 400 feet Goudhurst is one of the highest villages in Kent. From the fine vantage point held by St Mary's church, at the top of the High Street, you look out over the slopes which brought prosperity to the village. Sheep-rearing was prominent here, when 14th-century Flemish weavers brought their skills and made Goudhurst one of the foremost centres for high-quality broadcloth. The row of cottages opposite the church was once their Weavers' Hall. Other fine half-timbered and tile-hung houses rose during this period of prosperity. In the 16th and 17th centuries a different wealth came, this time from the iron industry. Then the

FOOD and DRINK

You should not miss the Star and Eagle, dating from the 14th century and possibly once part of an old monastery, which lies beside the churchyard at the top of the High Street. In a relaxed atmosphere, surrounded by old beams and beside the large inglenook fireplace, you can enjoy a wide range of dishes, with Brakspear, Flowers IPA and Flowers Original on the handpump (telephone: 01580 211512). There are other choices too. At the crossroads by The Plain stands the revamped Vine Hotel (telephone: 01580 211261)while two establishments provide teas, Squirrels Tea Rooms and Restaurant below the crossroads and Weeks Bakers and Caterers above the crossroads.

lower slopes beside the river Teise throbbed to the sound of hammer and forge. St Mary's church contains memorials to the different generations of the Culpeper family of Bedgbury Park who made much of their fortune this way.

The walk starts from the centre, The Plain, at the crossroads by the pond, and takes you along the north-western slopes above the river Teise. Sheep still graze here and, in the distance, you see some of the hop gardens which also characterise this area. You then walk gently up the slope again above the valley and move onto land which once formed part of the Bockingfold estate. When you return to the village you pass the site where in Tudor times a beacon was maintained nearby, ready to be lit in times of war. As you walk down the High Street you pass the site of fierce battles between the Hawkhurst gang of smugglers and the militia.

THE WALK

❶ With the war memorial to your left and the Vine Hotel to your right, walk north along the B2079 for 50 yards. Just before Clarkes Estate Agent turn left along the footpath signed to Trottenden. Walk down a narrow path flanked by a fence and a hedge. Cross a stile and follow the path downhill through pasture to a pair of oak trees. Ahead you have a superb view of the Wealden countryside, with fields and woodland interspersed with oast houses. The river Teise winds its way northwards below you and Horsmonden church lies in the middle distance on the further slope. Walk to the far right-hand corner of the next field. Cross a stile set in the hedgeline and follow the path between trees to a stile leading onto a narrow lane. Cross into the field opposite you and continue over pasture, leaving a private tennis court to your right. Cross a stile then turn right along a small road towards Trottenden Farm.

❷ At a grass triangle turn left along a gravel drive. Bear right past a converted granary. Cross a stile and follow a fenced track across pasture. When the fencing

PLACES of INTEREST

Finchcocks, a remarkable Georgian manor built in 1725, stands 1 mile west of Goudhurst. It houses a fine collection of around 80 historical keyboard instruments, such as chamber organs, virginals, harpsichords, clavichords and numerous pianos, often played when the house is open (telephone: 01580 211702). Bedgbury Pinetum, to the south, contains the national conifer collection and makes an attractive place for walking at will or following waymarked trails. You will find the main car park beside the B2079 (telephone: 01580 211044).

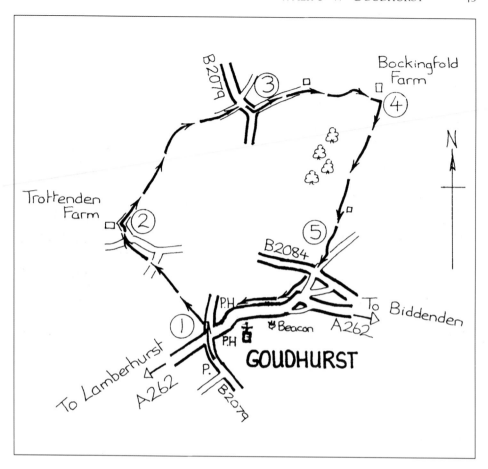

ends cross the next field to a stile set between two gates. Continue ahead, leaving to your left a deep well above one of the many springs typical of this area, then continue beside fenced woodland. Cross a stile and walk along a path between trees for 30 yards. At the edge of a meadow, turn right along the headland. Cross a stockproof bridge at the far right-hand corner of the field. Turn right and follow the headland for 100 yards to a stile. Cross the stile and follow the track through woodland. Another stile leads you ahead along a gravel track to the road.

❸ Turn right and walk for 100 yards. Turn left along a bridleway. Follow this for 600 yards to a private gateway at the end of the track. Here turn right. Walk along a field headland, beside a tall hedge on your left. Turn left, then right and walk downhill, leaving a poplar windbreak to your left. At the bottom of this small valley go over a field bridge. Bear left, then right and walk uphill towards the three oasts at Bockingfold Farm.

Bockingfold Farm.

❹ Turn right along a farm track, leaving a windbreak to your left. Go ahead, through a line of low bollards. After 700 yards turn right onto a tarmac driveway and continue to the road.

❺ Turn right and walk to the junction with the B2084. Cross, then go down the narrow road ahead. Bear right at a junction and continue to the main road (A262). Turn right and walk along the pavement back to Goudhurst with the sandstone tower of St Mary's church showing above the trees ahead.

WALK 9

UPPER UPNOR

Length: 5 or 6¼ miles

Really only a hamlet since it has no church of its own, Upper Upnor must be one of the smallest of its kind. It has one short street, barely 250 yards long, which runs down the slope to the banks of the river Medway, flanked by 17th and 18th-century weatherboarded houses. From the top you look directly down to the sailing craft which frequent this stretch of the river. At the bottom you find, to your right, a look-out tower, to your left, Upnor Castle. This fortification was built between 1559 and 1567 to defend Her Majesty's ships from attack as they lay at anchor in the upper reaches of the Medway. Until that time no village existed on the site and the Treasurer of Marine Causes paid the owner of the land £25 for the six acres taken to build the defence. The anchorage grew during the next hundred years. Dockyards developed on St Mary's Island opposite and Chatham became a focal point for the Navy. Sadly, the castle at Upnor failed to repel a fierce attack by the Dutch in 1667.

This walk takes you downstream to Lower Upnor. This mainly grew in the 19th century as a holiday resort. Today it is much used by sailors and is now home both to sprit-sail barges and faster modern boats. You then walk up the slope and continue on high ground, with good views

over the Medway. On a clear day you can see Sheerness and the Isle of Sheppey. You return by boatyards and along the shore where you get the full flavour of this active sailing area. You will find much to enjoy in the different kinds of sailing craft to be seen on the water. With Upnor Castle ahead, and the old Naval Dockyard on the far shore, the history of this important waterway comes to life.

If you start from Lower Upnor you reduce the walk by 1 mile, making the distance either 4 miles or 5¼ miles, depending on whether you include the stretch east of Hoo St Werburgh.

THE WALK

Please note that the 2½ mile stretch beside the river Medway as you return on this route cannot be walked 1 hour either side of high tide. For details of tides please con-

Thames barges at Hoo Marina.

tact the Riverside Services Management, Medway Ports, Sheerness Docks, telephone: 01795 561234.

❶ From Upper Upnor turn right from the car park entrance. Cross the road leading into Upper Upnor. Turn left along a footpath. Go down steps to the road leading into Lower Upnor. Bear right, then walk ahead along the road, passing an old military depot, then boatyards, on your right. Bear right at the post and telephone boxes opposite the Pier public house to walk along the front.

❷ Turn left at an obelisk set up in honour of sheriffs, and a stone dated 1204 beside it. Walk up the hill ahead of you, following the Saxon Shore Way sign. When you see wooden steps set in the hillside ahead,

turn right. Turn left after a second set of steps, continue up a gravel path, then walk along the road. After 250 yards take a right-hand turn along a narrow lane, following the footpath between fence and wall. Continue as this becomes a metal track with a hedge to your left and a broad field to your right. You now see the Medway beyond. Ahead rises the power station at Kingsnorth on a site which was once a royal hunting ground and where airships were built in the First World War.

At Cockham Farm bear right round an area of grass, then continue along a metalled drive. A metal barrier across the path is not intended to deter walkers. You now see the spire of the church of St Werburgh at Hoo St Werburgh. Soon you see Hoo Island, with Hoo Fort and Folly Point. Continue past a first group of houses. At a

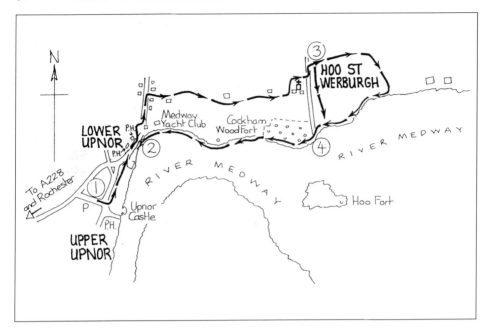

second set of houses, level with the church, turn left along a headland path, leaving a tall hedge to your right. Turn right at end of the garden and walk along a narrow path to St Werburgh's church. The dedication is to the daughter of the King of Mercia, who founded a nunnery here in Saxon times. Continue past the church to the road. Turn left along the road for 100 yards. Cross the road just before the bend, then turn right along a metalled path, signed to the Country House Nursing Home.

❸ For the longer walk, continue for 800 yards, then turn right and walk down to the shore. Turn right and follow the sea wall along the shoreline beside the salt marshes until you reach a brick shed wall. Cross a stile then walk across tarmac to the start of boatyards.

For the shorter walk, turn right after 100 yards and walk along an old hedgeline between fields towards masts and spars. Go ahead along a broad tarmac entrance. At the building ahead turn right to the start of boatyards.

❹ Take the narrow path to the right of the entrance, going between a tall con-

---

PLACES of INTEREST

The gun fort at **Upnor Castle** has been well preserved. You can visit the fortification and see the towers, gun emplacements and parapets throughout the summer months (telephone: 01634 718742). The **Dockyard at Chatham** has been preserved as a fascinating museum where you can see the history of the Navy on this site, something of the famous ships built here and some of the older crafts now being revived (telephone: 01634 823800).

crete wall on your right and a metal fence on your left. Cross the entrance to The Hundred of Hoo Sailing Club. Continue along a narrow path between the sailing club fence and a shed. Turn left just beyond the gates of Hoo Marina. Where the path opens out bear left, leaving bungalows to your right and a shipyard to your left. At the Hoo Ness Yacht Club turn right, then left, to skirt a low blue building, then continue on your old heading. After 30 yards turn left. Follow a concrete path to Port Werburgh. Enter and walk ahead along the footpath by the water's edge. At the end of the marina walk down to the beach. As you walk along the shore you pass the ruins of Cockham Wood Fort, built after the defeat by the Dutch in 1667.

When you reach the end of the beach, go up onto the shore beside the Medway Yacht Club. Walk ahead to the road at Lower Upnor. You pass the Training Ship *Arethusa*, the fourth in a line first started by the Shaftesbury Homes in 1873. Walk along the road for 450 yards. Where the road bends right, go ahead up steps to return to Upper Upnor.

BENENDEN

Length: 2½ miles

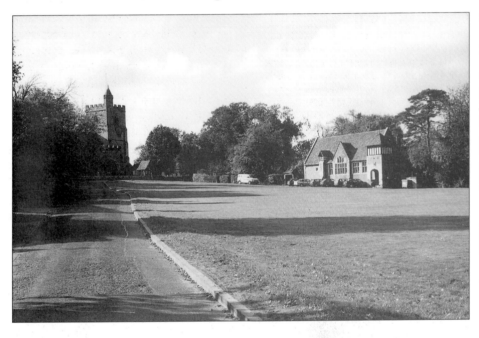

Getting there: Benenden is on the B2086, 6 miles west of Tenterden and 3½ miles south-east of Cranbrook.

Parking: You may park your car around The Green. If you are visiting one or other of the pubs you may park in their space, but please ask before leaving your car while you walk.

Maps: OS Landranger 188; Explorer 136 or Pathfinder 1250 (GR 808327).

At Benenden, church and lychgate, school, larger houses, stable with hayloft above all surround one of the largest and most attractive greens in the county. They suggest permanence and a long history. A church has certainly stood to the south of The Green since before Domesday. The present church of St George rose in the late 17th century after lightning totally consumed the earlier wooden building. Parishioners built the tower with the interest accrued on money from the sale of the scrap metal from the old bells. But most of the rest was designed or recreated by the architect George Devey, for Lord Cranbrook, in the 1860s. The area which acle and Passion plays there. In the 17th and 18th centuries bowls was the favoured game. By the 19th century, enlarged by the removal of an alehouse and cottages by the church, The Green became well known for the cricket matches still played there in the summer months.

The walk takes you from The Green beside the church, down Wealden slopes and over fields to the hamlet of Iden Green. A walk through orchards and along a woodland path take you on to the only pub now remaining in this little hamlet, the Woodcock Inn, a small, friendly place with low beams and an open fire. You then walk down a narrow metalled lane, flanked with trees, and return through woods and over a broad stretch of arable land from where you have superb views southwards

---

FOOD and DRINK

To the west of The Green, just along the main road, lies the 17th-century King William IV Inn. With inglenook fireplace and low beams, it has the full range of Shepherd Neame ales, and soups and pates worth walking four times the mileage to enjoy (telephone: 01580 240636). At Iden Green you find the Woodcock Inn, open seven days a week. This tiny public house, once a cobbler's shop, became an alehouse in 1798. Here beside the 17th-century fireplace, you can drink a local ale, Level Best from Northiam, as well as other good brews (telephone: 01580 240009). On your return you can try the Bull, to the east of Benenden's Green (telephone: 01580 240054).

became The Green has always drawn people to it. In the Middle Ages it may have seen wandering players perform Mir-

The Jubilee Memorial.

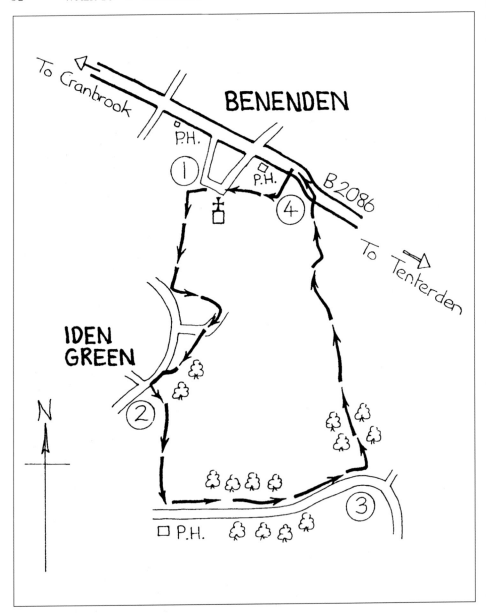

over the Weald towards the Rother valley. An easy walk crossing several sturdy stiles brings you back to The Green at Benenden with its choice of pubs.

THE WALK

❶ Turn right at the church lychgate along footpath 322. Bear left at the end of the wall and follow a metalled path towards a stile. Ignoring the stile, bear left and continue along the metalled path, going downhill, through two swing gates. Just before the road turn left between posts along footpath 324. Cross a tarmac path and continue between trees to a fence. Turn right and walk along a driveway. Where the drive turns right go ahead over a stile and walk between young trees to a field. Cross a stile and walk across the field to the far right-hand corner. Cross a stile onto a road. Turn left and walk up the road towards Iden Green.

❷ Just before buildings turn left. After 20 yards bear left under a pergola and walk along a well-trodden grass track to a stile. Cross the stile and bear right between apple trees. At the far side of the orchard turn left. After 25 yards turn right over a stile. Walk along the footpath beside a small sewage works then continue ahead along a concrete path to the Woodcock Inn. Turn left and walk along a pleasant, narrow road flanked by pollarded trees.

❸ At the bottom of the slope ignore the sign to footpath 333. Turn left 100 yards later just before a bridge. Cross a stile. Turn right to walk up the side of a field, leaving the fence to your right. At the top of the field cross a stile. Bear left between trees. Cross a stile and emerge from the woods then bear right up the side of the field. At the top right-hand corner cross a stile into woodland. Cross a stile and go over a small wooden bridge over a ditch. Bear left across the field to the far top left-hand corner from where you have a wonderful view southwards over the High

Weald. Leave the view and turn right along a broad farm track. After 150 yards turn left into a field. Bear right and continue in a straight line across three fields, crossing stiles, to the road.

❹ At the last stile turn left to walk along the road. After 150 yards turn left to follow a public footpath sign across a playing field. Aim for a gap between trees. Walk ahead then right going round two sides of a football field. Go through a swing gate and bear right through the churchyard to return to the lychgate where you began the walk.

SMARDEN

Length: 2½ miles

Getting there: Smarden lies 3½ miles north-east of Biddenden, 3 miles east of Headcorn and the A274, and 6½ miles south of the A20 at Charing.	Parking: Each pub has parking for those who are patrons, otherwise you will find space beside the road on the edge of the village.	Maps: OS Landranger 189; Explorer 136 or Pathfinder 1230 (GR 880423).

Smarden is a Wealden gem set beside the diminutive river Beult. Today it is little more than a village on two streets. St Michael's, a fine but massive church in the centre, forms the focal point. Edward III licensed Smarden as a market town in 1332 and it maintained a flourishing woollen industry for several centuries. The remarkable half-timbered building to the north of St Michael's, the old Cloth Hall, with hoist and doorways in one gable, recalls those days. Other fine half-timbered houses are also evidence of a wealthy past. One is Hartnup House, just north of the church, first built as a Wealden hall-house, then extended. The

FOOD and DRINK

You are spoilt for choice! In the centre of Smarden the 16th-century Chequers Inn offers excellent meals in pleasant, friendly surroundings. As well as other good ales you can expect a Rother Valley Brewery bitter and London Pride (telephone: 01233 770217). The tile hung and weatherboarded Bell at Smarden Bell makes a delightful alternative, although it is not on the route of the walk. Meals are varied and interesting while the range of ales seems endless: Harvey's Sussex Best, London Pride and Shepherd Neame Spitfire and Masterbrew (telephone: 01233 770283). Thirdly, but not least, the Flying Horse opposite the site of the old racecourse offers all the best of Shepherd Neame (telephone: 01233 770432).

arch of the doorway reveals roses of Lancaster and York carved sometime before 1485.

The walk is gentle, across open fields and through woodland of the Wealden plain. You pass several Wealden houses on your way, the most notable perhaps is Vesper Hawk House, for centuries the centre of a flourishing farm. On your return you cross one of the tributaries of the Beult, for it is in these meadows that this tributary of the Medway first forms itself, drawing on several streams which flow down from the Greensand Hills above.

THE WALK

❶ Set out from the little square to the south-east of St Michael's church, beside the Flying Horse. Cross the road and walk ahead along Beult Meadow, where the old racecourse lay. Continue along the path

Hartnup House.

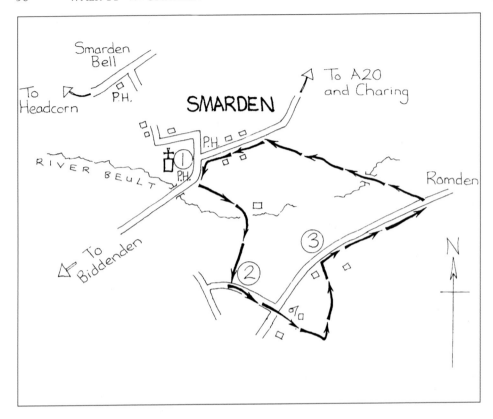

ahead of you and cross the stile. Follow the footpath to Buckman Green, bearing right across a field. Cross a stile beside a yellow marker post to the left of a metal gate. Follow the arrow across the next field towards the left-hand side of a granary at Vesper Hawk House. This fine house, with hung tiles above a brick understorey and interesting carving on the doorway, was first built at the end of the 15th century. Go through the gateway onto the farm drive, opposite garages. Turn right. Follow the farm track through a gate, leaving a garden fence to your left, and walk to a bridge. Go ahead in a direct line from the bridge across fields, to a small road.

❷ Turn left. Walk to a T junction at Golden Square. Here you will see, to your left, one of the many deep hollows which may have been formed as people dug for clay for building. Go ahead between Quince Cottage on your left and Summerfield on your right and follow a broad track for 250 yards. When this track bends right into hop gardens, go ahead along a smaller lane. Cross the stile to the left of a gate. Go over a broad wooden footbridge then walk ahead for 50 yards, leaving a pond to your left. Turn left, cross a bridge over a ditch, then bear slightly left across the field to a marker in the hedge. Go down steps and cross the stream, using stepping stones, then climb up to the path above. Follow the well-trodden track ahead between trees, using yellow markers as guides. Turn left along the headland of a hop garden. Continue, with a poplar windbreak to your left, and walk to a farm drive running at right-angles to your line. Cross the narrow bridge on the far side of the drive. Turn left down the headland and continue along a driveway to a road.

❸ Turn right and walk for 850 yards along the verge beside this quiet road until you reach a barn on your right. Turn left at a concrete footpath marker, cross a stile, turn at 45 degrees and walk to a pair of gates ahead. Go through the right-hand gate and walk ahead, leaving a fence to your left. Bear right after 350 yards and cross the tributary of the river Beult by a footbridge, the Gain Bridge, then bear right to a stile. Cross the stile, then follow the footpath along the headland to your left. After 400 yards go through a gateway or over a stile to its right and continue along the headland footpath. Cross a stile at the beginning of a brick wall and walk ahead, crossing a side road to reach the High Street in Smarden. Turn left. As you walk to the centre of the village you will pass a fine half-timbered house, Chessenden, and the Zion chapel, built in 1841 with classical front. One of the ways into the churchyard lies ahead of you at the turning in the road.

PLACES of INTEREST

West of Biddenden on the A262, the gardens at **Sissinghurst Castle** (National Trust) make a worthwhile visit. Created by Harold Nicholson and Vita Sackville-West, they cover 4 acres and provide a delightful sequence of plantings, beneath an Elizabethan gatehouse tower. The gardens are popular and access is controlled by timed tickets to avoid overcrowding (telephone: 01580 715330). The **Union Mill**, built in 1814, at Cranbrook, west of Biddenden, is the best surviving smock mill in the country. Here you can see it in full working order (telephone: 01580 712256).

PLUCKLEY

Length: 4 miles

Getting there: Pluckley lies 3 miles south of the A20 at Charing, on the Charing-Smarden road.	Parking: There is usually space in the village and beside the road.	Maps: OS Landranger 189; Explorer 136 or Pathfinder 1230 (GR 926454).

Pluckley, long ago Plucca's clearing, lies on the slopes of the Greensand Ridge, south-facing and self-contained. Its small square outside the Black Horse has become well known from the filming of H.E. Bates' *The Darling Buds of May*. In the surrounding countryside you see the orchards and agricultural land depicted in those scenes. You should not be alarmed by Pluckley's reputation as Kent's most haunted village. Tales of a phantom coach, a red lady grieving in the churchyard or a young father killed by a bowling pin may be excessive but they certainly do not detract from the friendly feeling as you enter the village. At the centre stands St Nicholas' church, its shingled broach spire visible to all the countryside around. It contains two fine parclose screens, one from the 15th century, the other from

FOOD and DRINK

The Black Horse, a Whitbread inn, is the obvious choice before you start the walk or on your return. It is large and rambling inside but has many cosy corners and a huge inglenook fireplace. The food is good and there is plenty of it (telephone: 01233 840256). The Swan at Little Chart, built in the 15th century but with Dering 'lucky' windows added in the 19th century, is smaller but just as welcoming and friendly. It makes an excellent alternative or, indeed, additional watering place (telephone: 01233 840702).

1635. You will also see memorial brasses to the Dering family who lived here for many centuries. The exploits of some are slightly exaggerated. The reputation of the most distinguished, Sir Edward, a man of letters and member of parliament in the 17th century, lives in the windows you see throughout the one-time Dering estate. A Royalist, Sir Edward is thought to have fled the Roundheads in the Civil War by escaping through a window with an arch above it high enough for him to be able to leap. A later Dering had such 'lucky' windows introduced throughout the estate.

The walk takes you through three old manors of the parish and for a short while into the land of another parish, Little Chart. First you walk through orchards to reach Sheerland. This was once a rival manor to the Dering estate but, as the windows introduced even here reveal, the Derings eventually acquired it as their own. As you approach Little Chart you see vines growing again near where Romans first planted them in the 2nd and 3rd centuries. The shaped gables of East Kent also become a feature. At Little Chart you reach the valley of the Great Stour, still a tiny stream. Here the river has been

opened into mill ponds. You can see the mill where paper-making has flourished for two centuries. You pass St Mary's church, a post-war building erected to replace an old church, over ½ mile away, which was bombed in the Second World War. From Little Chart you rise to Little Chart Forstal, where H.E. Bates lived from 1931 until 1974. You return by Rooting Manor, another of the old estates of Pluckley parish, then, finally, pass Surrenden Dering, the home of Sir Edward and his descendants until fire destroyed the building in 1952.

THE WALK

❶ Turn right from Pluckley village onto the main road. After 120 yards turn right, following the Greensand Way footpath sign. Walk across a playing field to a gap in the hedge 50 yards from the right-hand side. Continue between apple orchards with a windbreak on your right, then along a broad sandy path with a tall hedge on your left. Pass Sheerland House. Cross a metalled track and continue ahead, bearing slightly left. Continue to a gate. Cross a metalled lane and continue, beside a tall brick wall. Cross a stile. Continue over stiles to a battered swing gate in old walls. Walk ahead along a broad track. Cross a

PLACES of INTEREST

Naturalists will enjoy **Hothfield Common** which is a unique feature East Kent. Here a sandstone plateau lying on impermeable clay has resulted in part heathland, part peat bog. The common is classed as a National Nature Reserve and a SSSI and supports a wide range of plant and insect life. It can be reached to the east of Little Chart.

The village centre, with St Nicholas' church in the background.

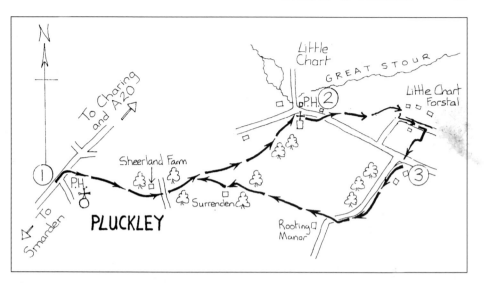

shingled track then go over a particularly tall stile in a windbreak. Turn left and follow a grass path beside the windbreak. Turn right after 75 yards. At the next corner cross a stile. Walk ahead down a broad path to a marker post. Continue to a gap at the far end of a brick wall. Go down steps to the road. The Swan at Little Chart stands opposite.

❷ Turn right along the road, leaving the church of St Mary the Virgin on your right. Just after the entrance to Gate Cottage cross the road. Go over a stile. Follow the Greensand Way diagonally right up a field, keeping to the left of a lone oak. Cross a stile. Turn right and walk along a field edge to a stile. Cross a small bridge. Bear left. Turn right at a garden end and continue along a farm track. Go through a gate after 50 yards. Continue along a metalled track past a house and gardens. Turn left onto the road and The Green at Little Chart Forstal. Just past The Green turn right over a stile. Cross this and walk down the right side of a field for 75 yards. Continue round the paddock to a hedge. Cross the stile. Turn left and walk down the field edge. Cross a stile onto the road.

❸ Turn right, then take the first turning on your left. Continue along the metalled lane for ½ mile to Rooting Manor. When the road swings left, turn right, doubling back to a stile in the fence. Cross this. Turn left and walk along a field headland. At the end of the fence bear diagonally right between trees. Go through a windbreak and continue to a gateway. Turn right, then, after 20 yards, left over a stile. Bear right, following the yellow arrow. Walk for 400 yards, then turn right up a broad path to the left of a windbreak. You can see to your left the cupola of Surrenden Dering. Follow the track left to gates and then onto a farm track. Opposite an old granary turn right through a metal swing gate. Bear left across a field to a stile in the wall. Turn left and retrace your steps to Pluckley.

APPLEDORE

Length: 6½ miles

Getting there: Appledore lies on the B2080, 5¼ miles south-east of Tenterden and 6 miles north-east of Rye, Sussex.	Parking: You may park beside the road along the main street, but be sure not to block the exits to driveways.	Maps: OS Landranger 189; Explorer 125 or Pathfinder 1250 and 1271 (GR 957294).

Set along one main street, Appledore, the village at the Apple Tree, sums up peace and calm. Many of the houses are half-timbered or protected by hung tiles dating from the 16th and 17th centuries. Spring blossom and autumn leaves bring this interesting old village further colour. Warmth and light are enhanced by the wide skies of the Romney Marsh to the south and east. This peaceful scene belies a stormy past. In medieval times, the river Rother flowed, as now, below the ragstone outcrop on which Appledore already stood, leaving it open to fierce attack first by the Danes in Saxon times, then by the French in the 13th century. By Tudor times weekly and annual fairs combined with local agriculture to bring prosperity.

FOOD and DRINK

There is plenty of scope for refreshment in Appledore and more along the way. The Swan Hotel, offers traditional ales and a filling range of meals (telephone: 01233 758329). At the Black Lion, you find Pilston Export and Beamish Irish Stout alongside local fish and game or Romney Marsh lamb pie (telephone: 01233 758206). At Warehorne, the Woolpack Inn provides a pleasant break in its old surroundings (telephone: 01233 733888). There are two good tea rooms, Bayleaves (telephone: 01233 758208) on the east side of the street and the Appledore Tea Room by the old market square (telephone: 01233 758272).

The open space where the fair was held beside St Peter's church still remains. The Royal Military Canal, built in the early 18th century to defend the country from attack by Napoleon, helped Appledore further for it drained the marsh and so removed the scourge of malaria.

The walk takes you beside the Royal Military Canal, along the route of the ancient river Rother where Viking long-ships once sailed. To your right stretch The Dowels, the lowest-lying part of Romney Marsh. Further on you see above you first St Mary's church, Kenardington, then St Matthew's church at Warehorne. Both these church towers often served as look-outs over the Marsh. Soon you walk up the slope, once the old cliff line, to the tiny village of Warehorne. Here smugglers hid their contraband, escaping the militia by a tunnel which ran between inn and church. You then return over fields along the top of the old cliff line. On a clear day

St Matthew's church, Warehorne, with its brick porch and shaped gable.

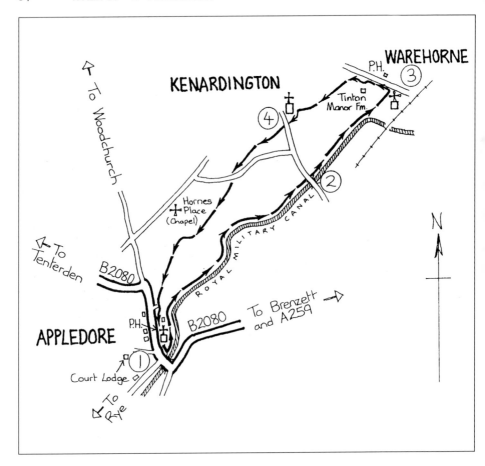

there are extensive views over Romney and Walland Marshes.

THE WALK

❶ Walk down the main street of Appledore, leaving St Peter's church to your left. Continue down the narrow road leading from the old market square. Just after the junction with the old Military Road, signed to Iden Lock and Rye, turn left through a swing gate onto National Trust land. Go onto the raised embankment and walk beside the canal for 2½ miles.

❷ Cross a road and continue until you see St Matthew's church, Warehorne, in line with a pylon. St Mary's church, Kenardington, built on the site of a Saxon encampment, stands above you on your left. After ¼ mile where the canal swings right look for a marker post placed on your right-hand side. Follow this to your left through the hedge, crossing a stockproof bridge and a stile. Turn right beside a farm track then bear left up the hillside towards the church. Cross the stile into the churchyard. Turn left along the church

The Saxon Shore Way between Kenardington and Appledore.

path to reach the road. Turn left.

❸ Pass the Woolpack Inn on your right. Turn left after 200 yards into the entrance to Tinton Manor Farm. Almost immediately turn right through a gate and continue ahead over two fields. In the second field, make for a marker post and stile to the right of taller trees. In the far distance you see the tower of the church of All Saints at Woodchurch. Cross the stile, then turn left immediately, over another stile. Walk down to a stile in the far right-hand corner of a field. Here the right of way should take you ahead to a series of three bridges over dykes. However, field patterns are changing so follow the sign across the stile. When you reach the first dyke turn left to reach the first of the

bridges. Cross the three bridges, bear slightly right and head uphill to a double stile at the top of the field. Cross, then continue uphill, crossing two more stiles, to reach St Mary's church, Kenardington. Here you climb a short, steep bank, once defences for Saxon defence works. Walk to

---

PLACES of INTEREST

Hornes Place, on the road to Kenardington, contains a chapel built and licensed for private worship in 1366, open (English Heritage) by arrangement (telephone: 01304 211067). At Brenzett, along the B2080 to the east, the **Aviation Museum**, run by the Aeronautical Museum Trust, contains wartime memorabilia (telephone: 01233 627911). At the **Rare Breeds Centre** at Highlands Farm, Woodchurch you can see 55 rare British animal breeds (telephone: 01233 861493).

the far left-hand corner of the churchyard. Turn left over a stile, then right to follow the path to the road.

❹ Bear left across the road, cross a stile and walk ahead until you reach a stile leading into a paddock. Cross the paddock. Walk ahead through a deep ghyll, crossing stiles, to reach a field on the far side. Bear left and continue for 75 yards to steps and a stile leading onto the road. Cross the road, then bear right across a field, towards the right-hand of two pairs of trees. Cross a narrow bridge, then walk ahead up two fields. Walk beside a hedge for 200 yards, then, at a stile set in the fence to your right, bear left and walk over a mound, going between two trees. Continue downhill to the far left-hand corner of the field, then cross a stile. Walk to the far left-hand corner of the next field. Here cross a narrow bridge and a stile into another field, then bear diagonally left to the far hedgeline. Turn left and walk along the headland until you reach a gate on your right. Go through this, then cross the playing field to the far corner by the road. Turn left and continue for ¼ mile to the centre of Appledore.

GREAT CHART

Length: 4½ miles

| **Getting there:** 1 mile south of Ashford take the turning to Great Chart from the A28, the Ashford to Tenterden road. | **Parking:** You will normally be able to park beside the road in the village. Alternatively, there is a small car park at The Street, opposite St Mary's church. | **Maps:** OS Landranger 189; Explorer 137 or Pathfinder 1230 (GR 983420). |

Great Chart sits on a hill above the Great Stour, with one main street and a peaceful aspect. In Saxon times this was the main town in the region until marauding Danes raided the area and reduced it almost to rubble. From then on Ashford, the settlement at the river crossing, overtook it in importance. To some degree, however, Great Chart's fortunes revived. The slopes provided valuable grazing land and for several centuries the monks of Christ Church, Canterbury, relied on wool from sheep of Great Chart for their clothing. In addition, the townspeople held a weekly market and an annual fair on land below the church.

FOOD and DRINK

From outside the Swan sums up some of the
history of Great Chart. Hung tiles and brick cover
the old timbering of a 16th-century building on one
side. The other has the shaped gables you come
to expect in this village. Inside you find the full
range of Whitbread ales, good food an old
atmosphere and a timelessly friendly welcome
(telephone: 01233 623250).

Today, as you walk up the main street,
you find many of the houses distinguished
by the shaped gables typical of East Kent.
Among them you can see a row of three
almshouses first built in 1583 by Francis
Toke of Godinton and rebuilt, as the
inscription shows, with gables, in 1833, by
Toke descendants. You can see memorials
to the Toke family in the fine ragstone
church of St Mary the Virgin which stands
at the top of the village. Particularly
intriguing is the one to Captain Nicholas
Toke who died aged 93, while returning, it
is said, from London, with the lady he
intended as his third wife. Near to the
church, at the gateway, stands a small half-
timbered building which has perplexed
many. Sometimes called the Pest House, it
may have been in reality a priest's house.

The walk takes you for a short way up
Chart Avenue, the old route to the Tokes'
house at Godinton, then goes alongside
the Great Stour itself. This small river rises
in the North Downs near Lenham, then
runs through Canterbury and Fordwich,
the ancient port of Canterbury, before
meeting the sea beyond Sandwich. You
then cross low-lying land to pass near to
Hothfield, a neighbouring parish, before
returning over the land of Godinton Park.

After heavy rain, you may prefer to
avoid the low-lying ground beside the
Stour. To do this, take the left turn along
the country road beside the Swan. Follow
the road for 1 mile. Turn right over the
railway and walk for another 1½ miles to
join the route at point 4.

THE WALK
❶ Walk along the main street, passing
the Swan on your left. Cross the side road
and bear left to follow the broad path
which leads past the cricket pitch. Turn
left after ½ mile and follow the signs for
the Stour Valley Walk down to the Great
Stour. Cross the river and continue to the
road above Worten Mill. Turn left onto
the road and continue.

❷ Just after the sign for Southern Water
Services turn right over a stile. Turn sharp
right and walk across the field to the far
side. Cross two stiles set close together at a
double fence and go up some steps. Go
over an embankment and down steps.
Cross a stile and bear right to a stile in a
low fence. Cross the stile, then, after 10
yards, cross a sturdy field bridge over a
stream. Continue on the same line, crossing stiles until you come to a farm track.
Here turn right.

PLACES of INTEREST

The Toke family held **Godinton Park** from 1440 until
1895. The red-brick house, with shaped gables
outside and superb panelling inside, was built in
1628 for Captain Nicholas Toke, whose brass rests
in the North Chapel at St Mary's church. It
contains collections of fine china and furniture.
The house is open to the public occasionally in the
summer months (telephone: 01233 620773).

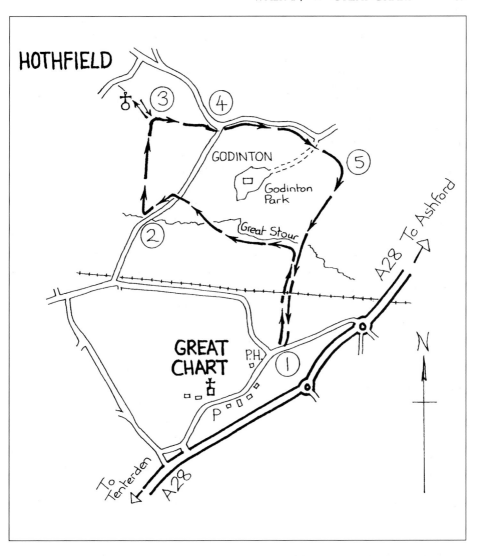

❸ After 20 yards go through a gate. If you turn left here and follow signs up the field you will reach St Margaret's church, Hothfield, whose tower and shingled spire were built in the 17th century after lightning had destroyed the earlier church. To continue the walk, turn right at the gate and walk down the right-hand side of the field for 200 yards. Bear left and walk to a bridge over a stream. Cross, then follow the path up the hillside, over a rough metalled track, to the far left-hand corner.

❹ Cross the road to steps opposite. Walk to a field corner, then bear left. Walk along the headland, leaving hedge and

Almhouses in Great Chart.

road to your left. Continue into woodland and follow the path to a stile into a field. Continue to a metal kissing gate in the far fence, then cross the drive which leads to Godinton House. Go through the gate opposite and walk ahead to the next gate.

❺ Turn right. Follow the headland beside a tall hedge for 250 yards. Turn right through a large gateway and follow the headland along the upper side of the field. Turn right on the farm track between shaws, then go through a metal kissing gate. Walk diagonally across two fields. Bear left. Pass a house on your left then walk towards a broad farm track. Cross this and follow Chart Avenue downhill, over the railway, and past the cricket field. Bear right to The Street at Great Chart. Cross the side road and return past the Swan.

HERNHILL

Length: 3½ miles

Getting there: To approach Hernhill from the west leave the M2 or A2 at junction 7 of the M2. Take the A2 as for Dover but turn left immediately to Boughton Street. At Boughton Street turn left, right, then left again to reach Hernhill. From the north-east (A299) turn left for Mount Ephraim Gardens and Hernhill.

Parking: You may park by the roadside or use the car park beside the Red Lion if you are visiting the pub.

Maps: OS Landranger 179; Explorer 149 or Pathfinder 1211 and 1195 (GR 065607).

One way to enjoy this delightful village is from the seat beneath the oak tree on the green. Flanked on one side by an old Wealden hall-house, now the Red Lion, on another by the old manor house and a row of gabled cottages, on the third by the church of St Michael, the setting is ideal.

On a hot summer day there is a cooling breeze from the sea barely three miles away. Once only a chapel stood where St Michael's church now stands, visited by pilgrims on their way to Canterbury. The present church, entirely Perpendicular in style, was built as a thanks-offering for the safe return of local men from Agincourt. For centuries Hernhill, like the neighbouring villages of Dunkirk and Blean, remained isolated from the world, something of an outback, though so near to Canterbury. The village made headlines in 1838 when some local men joined a protest march, led by 'Mad' John Tom, alias William Courtenay. They demanded food and an improvement to their living conditions. As the men bore arms the militia was summoned. Courtenay fired and the encounter left twelve men dead. Eight of the rebels are buried in St Michael's churchyard, where a plaque commemorates what became known as the Battle of Bossenden Wood.

The walk takes you through some of the woods, now peaceful, on the slopes above Hernhill. To reach them you walk across fields, until recently orchards but now arable land. A short stretch along quiet roads takes you to the start of the woodland walk. From here, as you rise up the slope, you see the old harbour of Whitstable, on the North Kent coast, and Shell Ness at the eastern point of the Isle of Sheppey. Beyond the Isle of Sheppey you

see shipping on its way to and from the river Thames. When you leave the woods, another narrow country road reveals more views, this time over The Swale, towards the Isle of Harty. For much of the way you look down on Hernhill. The beacon turret on the tower of the church recalls the time when these slopes above the coast provided an important role in relaying messages of invasion. The return takes you through extensive orchards.

THE WALK

❶ Leave The Green and the Red Lion to your right and continue along the road for 300 yards. Just after the last house on your right, turn right and walk along a narrow, fenced path. Cross a stile, then bear diagonally left towards a stile in the hedgeline. Cross this and continue to a stile above a road. Turn right and walk along the road for another 300 yards, then turn right up Crockham Road.

❷ Where the road swings right, continue ahead up a gravel track towards woodland above you. Ignore a right-hand path and follow the main track around the hillside and between trees for ½ mile. When you come to a division of ways, ignore the broader track which goes ahead. Instead

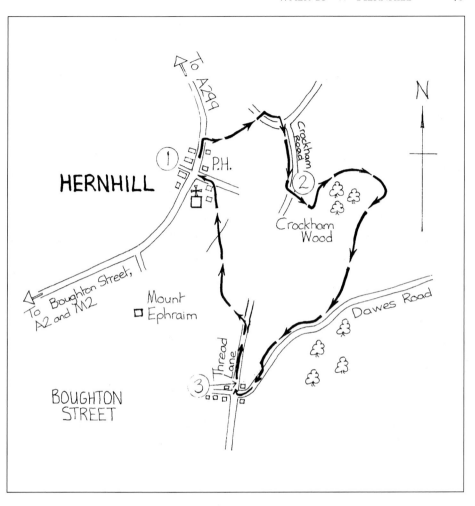

fork right along a narrower path. You will see self-seeded rhododendrons, as well as the beech, chestnut and oak of mixed woodland. Continue on this path, ignoring all tracks to left and right, then emerge from the woodland and walk ahead to reach Dawes Road after 650 yards. Turn right and walk downhill to the village of Boughton Street.

❸ Turn right along Thread Lane. After

500 yards, just before the woodland on your right comes to an end, turn left through a farm gateway. Walk along a broad track below orchards. Go ahead through a large metal gate and follow the path on to a water trough beside a gate. Here turn right and walk up the bank to a stile. From here you can look back to see Mount Ephraim House between trees. Cross the stile, bear left and walk through orchards. Cross a broad farm track and

In 1838, Hernhill made the headlines and this plaque commemorates the event.

continue to a stile in a windbreak. Cross and turn left, then after 30 yards turn right at a yellow marker. Walk up a broad, grassy swathe between pear trees. After 200 yards turn right. Walk for 60 yards, then turn left and cross a narrow stockproof bridge set in a poplar windbreak. Turn right along the headland. At the road turn left and walk the last 250 yards back to Hernhill.

HASTINGLEIGH

Length: 3½ miles, with a further circular walk of 1 mile to visit the church

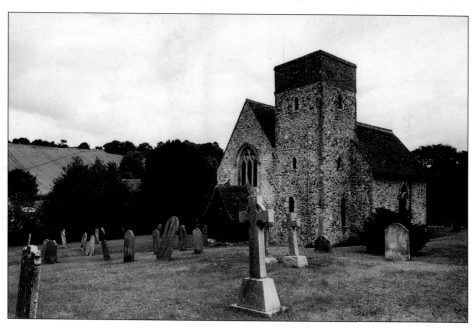

Getting there: Hastingleigh is 3 miles east of Wye. From junction 9 of the M20, take the A28 to reach Wye, then follow Coldharbour Lane to Wye Downs and continue to Hastingleigh. From junction 11 take the B2068 (Canterbury road) to the turning for Stelling Minnis. Hastingleigh is 3 miles to the west.

Parking: You may park in the village street and beside St Mary's church. There is also a car park on the road above Wye Downs.

Maps: OS Landranger 179; Explorer 137/138 or Pathfinder 1231 (GR 096449).

Like many small villages set high on the North Downs, surrounded by pasture and arable land, Hastingleigh remains isolated. It is a village in two parts, one the community on the brow of the hill, where some of the houses date from the 15th century, the other the little church, St Mary the Virgin, with Court Lodge beside it, nestling in a fold below. Sometimes inaccessible in winter snow, the atmosphere in and around the village is quiet and refreshing. Some say the name Hastingleigh refers to people who lived in a brushwood clearing, others that it describes the *leigh*, the clearing, of the Haestingas, or warlike people. The only known account of violence is a tale connected with the pond, known as the Witch's Pond, where, in 1799, youths once ducked an elderly woman. Today the pond has kindlier memories, with lime and plane trees, planted in 1897 for Queen Victoria's Jubilee, and a Coronation seat from 1953.

The walk takes you across fields and quiet lanes to a fine stretch of the North Downs above the scarp face. There are superb views towards Romney Marsh and the English Channel while, closer to you, the slopes of this Area of Outstanding Natural Beauty present a wonderful sight in spring and early summer with the many wild flowers of the chalk grassland. You pass The Devil's Kneading Trough, created after the last ice age when meltwater washed away the crumbling surface layers of chalk. Then you return to the village by lanes and fields. A further short walk leads you down to St Mary's church and back.

THE WALK

❶ With your back to the Bowl Inn, turn right, then right again at the junction, following the sign to Hastingleigh church and South Hill. Turn right after 200 yards. Walk across a field to a stile, cross and

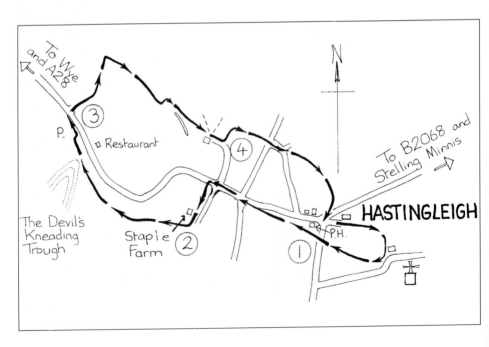

PLACES of INTEREST

A railway used to run up the Elham Valley, linking Canterbury with Folkestone. The **Elham Valley Railway Exhibition** at Newington, near Folkestone, describes the story of this line, with a full and extensive working model (telephone: 01303 273690).

make for the far left-hand corner of the field just before the crossroads. Turn left along the road. At the crossroads continue ahead for 275 yards to a smaller crossing at Folly Town. Here turn left. Walk past Staple Farm then past farm buildings at Cold Blow Farm. After 30 yards turn right over a stile and follow the sign for the North Downs Way. Here you have your first view over Romney Marsh.

❷ Keep to the left of a fallen hawthorn in a crater and make for a stile set between two gates. Cross the stile, go ahead and bear right along the fenceline. At the far side of this field cross a stile and turn left down a fenced path. Cross a stile and continue ahead. When you reach a gate bear right. Cross a stile and continue on the footpath, bearing uphill and away from the fence, then back to the top of The Devil's Kneading Trough. Turn right just before a gate. Walk to a swing gate, go through this, bear right, then go through another swing gate to reach a car park.

❸ Turn left at the road. After 100 yards turn right down a metalled lane for 500 yards. Turn right and walk along a field headland, leaving the hedge to your right.

The lychgate and church at Hastingleigh.

Continue round the edge of woodland to the top of the field, then turn left at a fence. Cross the stile ahead of you and walk up the right side of the next field. Turn right over a stile just before the top, then bear left above old coppice and make for a stile beside a gate. Cross the stile, then walk ahead above a fence for 100 yards. Now make for the top far left-hand corner of the field. Here cross one stile, then, after 50 yards, another, set in the fence to your right. Turn left along a metalled track.

❹ Where the track bends right, turn left. Follow the field headland beside a hedge to a line of well-spaced trees. Turn right and cross a field to a road. Walk ahead, following the sign to Hastingleigh and Elmsted. Where the road bends right go ahead over a wooden barrier into woodland and follow the path to a stile. Cross the stile, turn left and follow the field headland first beside woodland, then beside a hedge. When the hedge ends, continue ahead across the field to the corner of woodland. Continue to a T junction with a bridleway. Turn right to reach the road after 110 yards. Turn right again into Hastingleigh village.

To walk to the church, follow the lane beside the pond. Continue along a metalled track to a stile by The Vicarage. Cross and walk between trees for 400 yards. Just before a line of tall trees, turn right and walk down a field headland: first beside a hedge, then across an open field. Skirt farm buildings, leaving them to your left, and turn left onto the road beside a farm gate. To return, bear left beside the gate and walk diagonally up the field towards the right-hand corner of woodland. Skirt the woodland, leaving it to your left. Cross a stile and follow a grassy lane to the road. Turn right to Hastingleigh centre.

LYMPNE

Length: 2¾ miles

Getting there: Lympne is on the B2067, 1½ miles west of Hythe and 2 miles south of junction 11 of the M20.	Parking: There is a car park beside Lympne Castle, as well as the one for patrons beside the Country Members Hotel.	Maps: OS Landranger 179; Explorer 138 or Pathfinder 1252 (GR 121357).

There is a timeless feel to Lympne village as you stand at the end of Castle Close, beside its castle and its church. The village (pronounced Limm) takes its name from *Limen*, the Roman name for the river Rother which once flowed below it to the sea at nearby West Hythe. The 'p' of Lympne, never pronounced, first appeared in a medieval manuscript, perhaps by mis-

take. The old village, to the south of the main road, has grown over many centuries. In Roman times a watch tower stood where Lympne Castle now stands. Below lay steep cliffs and, at their foot, a harbour for the large fleet the Romans kept to hand. Romans also built a fortress halfway up the cliffs to protect the shore from invasion by the Saxons. Its walls, 20 feet

FOOD and DRINK

The Country Members Hotel stands beside the B2067 just round the corner from The Street. Cask ales on tap include Flowers Original and IPA, Sussex Best and Fuller's London Pride and two guest ales. There is plenty of space and the menu is varied (telephone: 01303 264759).

soldier still haunts the battlements. The castle was built for the Archdeacons of Canterbury. Thomas a Becket was just one of a series of priests who lived in Lympne Castle while Archdeacon. St Stephen's church was built about the same time. Its large Norman tower may well have been used as a look-out tower against invasion by the French and again when smugglers crossed the marsh with contraband.

wide in places, earned it the name Stutfall (Stout wall) Castle. Little now remains of all this might. The Roman harbour silted up, as did a newer harbour constructed further downstream at West Hythe. In 1285 a violent storm diverted the river Rother from its course, while gradually the fort, weakened by water seeping up from the rocks beneath, fell into ruins. All this time Romney Marsh encroached and was 'inned' for extra grazing land. In the 12th century the ruins of the watch tower gave way to Lympne Castle. It is said a Roman

The walk takes you along the old cliff top, giving splendid views over Romney Marsh, west towards the Hastings cliffs, and south to Dungeness and the English Channel. You then go down the slope of the old cliffs and walk beside the Royal Military Canal. The trees which line it provide welcome shade in summer. To return you walk up the slope, with the ruins of Stutfall Castle to your right and Lympne Castle, built with some of the stone from its 'stout walls', above you on

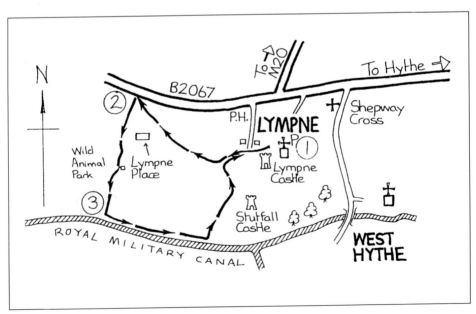

Lympne Castle.

the cliff top. From there you return along a track to Lympne Castle.

THE WALK

❶ From the car park beside Lympne Castle, walk past the castle entrance to the end of Castle Close. Turn left and walk between walls along a sandy, tree-lined track, signed for the Saxon Shore Way. Bear right. You soon have an extensive view of the Romney Marsh ahead of you and below you. In the distance to your left you can see Dungeness while immediately below lie the ruins of Stutfall Castle. Continue along this path, ignoring all turnings downhill. At a wooden horse barrier cross two lanes then continue along the lane ahead to a stile beside the main road.

PLACES of INTEREST

Lympne Castle, now a private home with its Great Hall restored and with an outstanding view over Romney Marsh, is open between June and September, from Monday to Thursday (telephone: 01303 267571). **Port Lympne**, also known as Lympne Place, built in 1915 in Cape Dutch style for Sir Philip Sassoon, has exotic touches such as a Moorish patio and an Egyptian frieze. Inside you can see the mural room painted with Asian birds and wildlife. Outside, where from 1973 John Aspinall created a wildlife park, you can see gorillas and rhinos, monkeys and tigers. Open daily, except Christmas Day, from 10 am to dusk (telephone: 01303 264646). At the top of Lympne Hill you can see the **Shepway Cross**, a war memorial to those who died from the Cinque Ports in the 1914-18 war. This stands on the site of the old meeting place for members of the Confederation of the Cinque Ports.

❷ Cross the stile and turn left down a metalled track. You soon approach the Port Lympne Wild Animal Park. At a large iron gate saying 'Danger: Wild animals. No public entry' turn left in front of it and go along a less well used metalled track. Turn right at another gate and walk, between animal pens, down a grassy track. Continue downhill to a small wooden bridge.

❸ Cross the bridge and take the path immediately on the left which runs just beside the zoo fence and is signed for the Royal Military Canal footpath. After 450 yards follow the canal path left then right as it bends for one of the canal's kinks or 'enfilades'. These were built, before the trees grew up, to allow gunfire to cover each length of the canal in case the enemy tried to cross. After another ½ mile turn left. Cross a narrow bridge over a drainage dyke, then continue ahead, then left to follow the path uphill. You can see the remains of Stutfall Castle to your right, while, higher still, Lympne Castle dominates the skyline. Climb a short flight of steps to the track by which you first set out. Bear right and return to the village.

WICKHAMBREAUX

Length: 3 miles

Getting there: Wickhambreaux lies 4¼ miles east of Canterbury and 1 mile north-east of the A257 at Littlebourne. You can reach the Littlebourne junction by taking the Patrixbourne/ Littlebourne turning from the A2, 2 miles south-east of Canterbury.

Parking: There is some parking to the right of Grove Road, north- east of the village. You may also park beside The Green.

Maps: OS Landranger 179; Explorer 150 or Pathfinder 1196 and 1212 (GR 220588).

Wickhambreaux was once an important stopping place on the way to the ferry over the Great Stour at Grove. It lies in the centre of orchards and fertile arable land, an immaculate village, set round a peaceful village green. The name recalls the time when the Stour was a broad tidal estuary and this was a small village (*wic*) in a water meadow (*ham*). The suffix-*breaux* was added in 1285 when William de Breuse or Braose owned the manor. At the time of Domesday Book the village flourished, its riverside pastures supporting three hundred sheep and thirty-one beasts. Then there were two water mills. Both Wickham Court on the far side of The

FOOD and DRINK

The Rose Inn (telephone: 01227 721763), in the centre of the village, was a 14th-century hall-house. A welcoming log fire still burns in winter in what was once the central fireplace. Excellent first courses include roast duck with raspberry and peppers and lamb cutlets to their own recipe. Ales include Fuggles and Wadworth 6X. Other opportunities for refreshment include The Tudor Cottage Restaurant in The Street while in Stodmarsh you pass the Red Lion pub (telephone: 01227 721339).

Green and The Old Rectory beyond appear Georgian but their 18th-century exteriors conceal medieval beginnings. At Wickham Court, once the manor house, according to tradition, Henry II met and wooed Rosamond Clifford, the 'Fair Rosa-

mond' of many tales. Two centuries later the manor was among those belonging to Joan Plantaganet, the grand-daughter of Edward I. Described as 'The Fair Maid of Kent', 'most beautiful woman in all the realm of England', she married the Black Prince. She may have lived in The Old Stone House, the oldest dwelling in the village, which stands at the south-east corner.

To the north-east of the village stands the 13th and 14th-century church of St Andrew. Its chancel arch bears medieval paintings of angels and flowers which had long been concealed under whitewash. Paintings on the walls of the north and south aisle are Victorian copies. The 'art nouveau' east window, the design of the Danish Arild Rosenkranz, was the first of its

The village green.

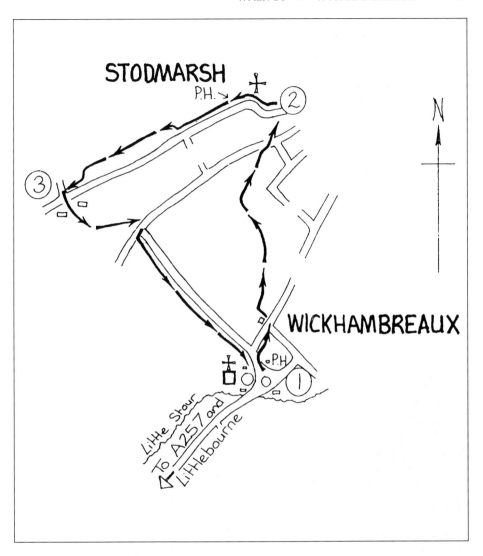

kind in England to be designed by a foreigner.

The walk takes you through orchards and across farmland to Stodmarsh. This tiny village lies between the Lampen Stream and the Great Stour to the north, beside marshland where the monks of Christchurch, Canterbury kept their *Stud* farm. The church of St Mary in Stodmarsh

has numerous fascinating features, from the rare wooden bell turret to crosses on the south-west door incised by Crusaders when they prayed before setting sail for the Holy Land. You then walk up from Stodmarsh along the ridgeway, a route much used by the monks as they went from Canterbury to Stodmarsh. From the top you have good views to north and south before returning by fields and a country road.

THE WALK

❶ Turn right from the Rose Inn and walk past The Old Rectory. Turn right along Grove Road. When you reach Quaives Farm go through the opening to the right of the gate. Walk up the left-hand side of an orchard. Cross a stile onto a metalled farm track. When the main track forks before a poplar windbreak continue ahead through a pear orchard. When you reach a fence, bear left along the headland. Go through a gate into a field, then bear right to the far corner, aiming for a telegraph post to the right of a church. At a T junction cross the road to a yellow marker post. Continue on the same heading across the next field, aiming just to the left of a telegraph post and a thatched cottage. Ahead to your left lies the village of Stodmarsh.

❷ Turn left onto the road and follow it to the village. Turn left at St Mary's church. Walk through the village and continue along the road for 600 yards. As you rise you see below the Westbere Marshes and Lake. The marshland at Stodmarsh forms an important National Nature Reserve and offers a wonderful bird spectacle in winter. Cross a stile in the fence to your right, then bear left and walk across the field just below a ledge, following the line

---

PLACES of INTEREST

Howletts Wild Animal Park (telephone: 01227 721286) provides a home for wild animals ranging from gorillas to elephants. It lies on the road from the A2 to Littlebourne and is open every day except Christmas Day from 10 am to dusk. At the **Wingham Bird Park** on the A257 towards Sandwich you can see a wide variety of otherwise endangered birds and small mammals (telephone: 01227 720836).

---

of the road above you. Cross a stile at the far corner and bear right along the road. Continue along the road for 100 yards.

❸ Turn left opposite a metalled lane, into the drive of Broadacres, and walk with discretion to the stile set to the left of the garage. Cross the stile and walk downhill. Ahead to your left you can see the towers of Richborough Power Station. Cross a stile and walk down the left side of a field. The old estate trees to your right are part of Trenley Park. At the bottom of the field turn left over a stile. Walk to another stile 10 yards ahead. Bear right to a bridge over the Lampen Stream, crossing first the bridge and then a stile. Bear left across a field to the far side. Follow a tractor track to a gateway then bear right to a stile leading onto the road. Go ahead down the road to return to Wickhambreaux. The spire you see ahead to your right marks St John the Evangelist's church in Ickham.

ST NICHOLAS AT WADE

Length: 3½ miles

Getting there: St Nicholas at Wade lies 8 miles west of Ramsgate, ½ mile south of the A299 and ¼ mile from the A28 north-east of Sarre.	Parking: You will find parking beside the two public houses and roadside parking to the east of them.	Maps: OS Landranger 179; Explorer 150 or Pathfinder 1164 (GR 265667).

The village of St Nicholas at Wade, a quiet corner in broad agricultural land, stands proudly above the stretch of flat land between the Isle of Thanet and the rest of Kent where at one time the Wantsum Channel ran. Here once the Roman fleet rode at anchor, sought a haven at the port at Sarre or sailed up to Fordwich, the port for Canterbury. In the Middle Ages the monks of Canterbury and

Chislet 'inned' what by then had become brackish marshland and reclaimed the land for pasture. The name Wade refers to the ford where people crossed the channel in the days before it finally shrank to a mere stream. St Nicholas' church, dedicated to the patron saint of sailors, was first a chapel of ease to St Mary's church at Reculver on the coast 3 miles away. Along with the twin towers at St Mary's, now all

FOOD and DRINK

The 17th-century Bell (telephone: 01843 847250), at the centre of the village, is a particular favourite, with its superb fish dishes, fresh crab and lobster. The regular real ales include Flowers IPA and Wadworth 6X. Guest beers such as Walsall and Footlights Ale change fortnightly. Opposite, the Sun Inn (telephone: 01843 847665) also has a wide range of ales and a variety of interesting dishes. Each pub has a good garden and plenty of space for children. At Sarre, off the route of the walk, you find the Crown Inn and the King's Head, while at Sarre Mill the tea rooms are open daily.

that survive there, St Nicholas' tower served as a landmark for far and wide. A house has stood on the site of St Nicholas Court since at least the 14th century. This is unique in having an underground chapel where, it is suggested, Lollards may have met. But the overall impression of the village is of buildings from the 16th and 17th centuries. Mellow brick buildings with stepped gables recall the influence of the Huguenot settlers who fled here from persecution in Tudor times.

The walk takes you through a wide landscape of open fields, intersected by drainage dykes. Today the dykes and fields offer a wonderful wildlife habitat. As well as St Nicholas' church tower, ever present on the skyline, you see Sarre Mill dominant to the south-west.

THE WALK

❶ Pass the Bell on your left, and walk past St Nicholas' church. As you pass the end of Shuart Lane you have your first view of the North Sea. Continue along Court Road, ignoring the left turn to St Nicholas Court, and take the flyover over

the A299. From this vantage point you have a clear view of the Reculver towers ahead beside the sea. Behind you to your left is the old Wantsum Channel. Turn left, following the sign to Potten Street. Ignore a right-hand turn and pass a thatched cottage called Nine Nails. Bear left. Continue along a metalled road, leaving the Wade Marsh Stream to your right.

❷ Turn right and cross back over the A299 by the flyover, then turn left and walk on the south side of the road, passing a narrow shaw on your right. Turn right down a bridleway marked to Wagtail Farm. Pass the Wagtail Farm entrance. Go ahead along an old metalled track and continue into woodland. Follow the track as it bends, first left, then right. Turn right beside the house at Belle Isle. Turn left, leaving the Wade Stream to your right. You soon see Sarre Mill ahead on the horizon. When you come to the farm at Down Barton walk to a stile beside a gate to the right of buildings. Cross the stile. Turn right, then walk along a concrete farm

PLACES of INTEREST

Sarre Mill lies on the north side of the A253, near the centre of Sarre village (telephone: 01843 847573). Rescued from decay and carefully restored in recent years, it is now open daily in summer and you can see this smock mill in full working order. You will find tea rooms and a farm shop, as well as a display of vintage agricultural machinery. **Quex House** at Birchington, to the north-east along the A28, houses the internationally renowned Powell-Cotton African and Asian collection. The house itself is a Regency mansion and stands in historic gardens (telephone: 01843 842168).

Sarre Mill.

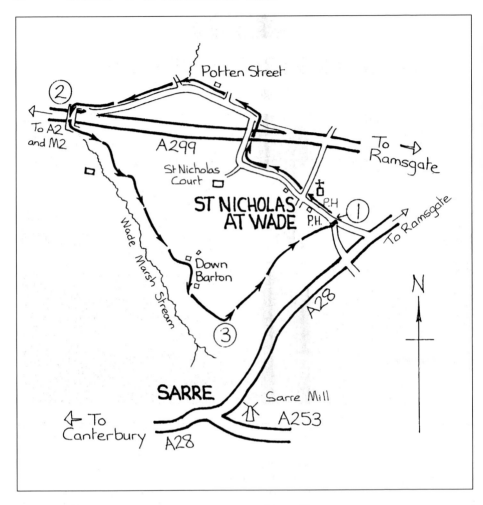

track, keeping Sarre Mill in your sight ahead of you. Cross a stream by a low concrete bridge and follow a broad track towards trees. Continue along the headland. The traffic you see ahead runs along the Sarre Wall.

❸ When you reach a swing gate on your right, turn left and follow the path uphill. It is well worth looking back as you near the top to see Sarre Mill on its outcrop, the course of the old Wantsum Channel below and the North Downs beyond.

Chislet, home of the monks who drained the marsh, lies ahead on the far slopes. The power station and wind generator to your left are at Richborough. When you reach houses continue ahead on a metalled path. Walk up the right-hand side of the playing field and bear right and follow the footpath through a short stretch of woodland. Bear right along a metalled path and go through a swing gate. Turn left at the road, then left again to return to the centre of the village and the two inns.

ST MARGARET'S AT CLIFFE

Length: 3 miles

Getting there: St Margaret's at Cliffe lies 1 mile off the A258 (the Dover to Deal and Sandwich road), 2 miles north of the junction of the A258 and the A2 and 3½ miles north-east	of Dover. **Parking:** There is one car park (24 hours) just beyond the church, another in the space (limited) beside the Dover	Patrol Memorial at Bockell Hill. You may also park at St Margaret's Bay. **Maps:** OS Landranger 179; Explorer 138 (GR 358448).

St Margaret's at Cliffe stretches along its one main street, just one mile from the cliffs beside the English Channel. People have lived here since early Anglo-Saxon times but the village grew in importance, as a resort, mainly in Victorian and Edwardian times. At the centre you will find the church of St Margaret of Antioch. First

built between 1130 and 1170 on the site of an earlier church, this is a wonderful example of Norman architecture. The doorway, with its carved medallions and dog-tooth patterns, is one of the finest and best preserved in Kent. Inside the church you will find, on the pillars of the nave, carvings of medieval ships. These may have been made by shipwrecked sailors who had been given shelter here.

The walk takes you above pasture in a quiet downland valley, then crosses arable land (National Trust) to the cliffs which overlook the English Channel. From here you can often see the coast of France. On a particularly clear day you may even see the clock tower at Dover. Ahead is the house from where coastguards kept watch over the straits of Dover, until they moved to the present coastguard station above Dover itself. You pass the 90 foot high obelisk erected as a memorial to the Dover Patrol, the sailors who, from their fleet of small boats, laid a minefield in the Channel in the First World War. Below, to the south, you can see St Margaret's Bay where smugglers used to roll ashore their kegs of brandy. Now it is a place for lobster pots and summer sports. If you want to extend the walk you can follow the signs for the Saxon Shore Way from beside the Old Coastguard Station and descend by the path and steps.

THE WALK

❶ Turn left out of the car park and walk along the footway beneath the church. At the church gate opposite the Cliffe Tavern cross the road and continue in same direction on the right-hand side of the road. Pass the village stores and also the post office. Turn right just before the Red Lion and walk along Kingsdown Road. When the road ends continue ahead along the chalk bridleway for ½ mile. You now see rolling downland to your left, while soon the Channel appears beyond Kingsdown through a cleft in the slopes. In early summer you will see the guelder rose, and later on sweet briar, growing in the hedgerows.

❷ When the main farm track goes on towards Kingsdown, fork right, following a circular walk sign along a narrower footpath. After 220 yards bear right. Continue between two broad fields, first downhill, then uphill, towards trees. Bear right towards the entrance to Bockhill Farm. Turn left and follow the path uphill, leaving a hedge to your right. Walk to a junction of tracks 100 yards from the cliff top.

❸ Turn right to pass the memorial, then bear right over a stile and follow a broad,

PLACES of INTEREST

The **Pines Garden** lies beside Beach Road, reached from the last bend off Bay Hill. Created in 1970, its six acres contain fine specimen trees and shrubs and house a statue to Sir Winston Churchill (telephone: 01304 852764). Opposite, the **Bay Museum** recounts the history of the area from the earliest days. The **South Foreland Lighthouse** (National Trust) provides another landmark on the cliffs. Built in 1843 to help navigation in the Channel, it was used by Marconi for his first radio communication in 1898 (telephone: 01892 890651).

The memorial to the Dover Patrol.

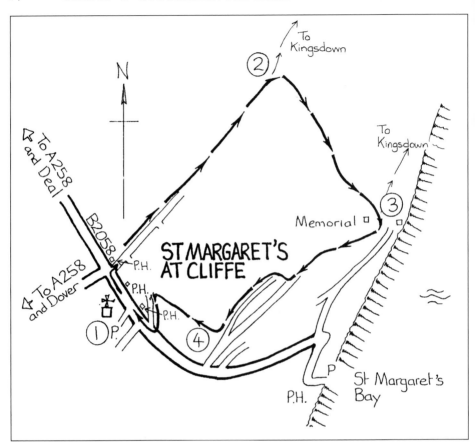

grassy track ahead of the gate to the far corner of the field. Go over a stile and walk along an unadopted road. Turn right just before the first house on your right, then left along another unmetalled road.

❹   After 400 yards turn right down a public footpath opposite the house called Kinver Edge. Cross a stile and walk down the left side of a field. Turn left at the bottom, over a stile, then turn right to walk up the right-hand side of a field, leaving a fence to your right. At the top, go ahead through an opening and walk up the left-hand side of the next field, leaving a hedge on your left. Turn left at the top of the field. Cross a stile and walk across the top of a large paddock, with a fence on your right. Cross another stile. Continue ahead with a fence on your right and trees to your left. Turn right along a concrete path and follow it round to a wider road. Bear left at a fork and continue to the road. Turn right at Sea Street in St Margaret's at Cliffe. The entrance to the car park and the church lie ahead on your left.